THE NELVANA STORY

NEIL—
NICE WORKING
WITH YOU! LET'S
GET BACK IN TOUCH—

THE NELVANA STORY
THIRTY ANIMATED YEARS

Daniel Stoffman

NELVANA.

Distributed in Canada by
Kids Can Press Ltd.
29 Birch Avenue
Toronto, ON M4V 1E2

Distributed in the U.S. by
Kids Can Press Ltd.
2250 Military Road
Tonawanda, NY 14150

www.kidscanpress.com

Produced by Denise Schon Books Inc.
Design: Joanna Kubicki
Editorial and proofreading: Judy Phillips, Julia Armstrong, Barbara Philps
Index: Barbara Schon

Back cover photo: Sandy Nicholson
Author photo: Paul Orenstein

Printed and bound in Canada by Friesens
PA 02 0 9 8 7 6 5 4 3 2 1

National Library of Canada
Cataloguing in Publication Data

Stoffman, Daniel
  The Nelvana story : thirty animated years

Includes index.
ISBN 1-894786-00-9

1. Nelvana (Firm) — History. 2. Animated films — Canada — History.
3. Motion picture industry — Canada — History. I. Title.

NC1766.C32N44 2001   384.8'06'571   C2001-902485-1

(ABOVE) THE ORIGINAL NELVANA. (OPPOSITE PAGE) PIPPI LONGSTOCKING BACKGROUND DRAWING. (PAGE 2) KING BABAR, FROM NELVANA'S SUCCESSFUL TELEVISION SERIES. (PAGE 6) FROM DONKEY KONG COUNTRY.

ACKNOWLEDGEMENTS

I want to thank the many Nelvanians who were so generous in sharing their memories and ideas with me. The three founders of the company, Michael Hirsh, Patrick Loubert, and Clive Smith, deserve special credit for insisting on a book that would tell the real story of Nelvana, one that would include not just the triumphs but also the mistakes, setbacks, and lapses of judgment. The result, I hope, is a credible and honest portrait of a great Canadian success story. I would also like to thank Peter Roe, who interviewed many of the animators who worked at Nelvana over the years and who generously shared this material with me. Denise Schon did a masterly job of organizing the project, and Joanna Kubicki found many imaginative ways to illustrate it. I am indebted to my in-house editor, Judy Stoffman, for her usual good advice and for coming up with a title.

Daniel Stoffman, February, 2001

CONTENTS

MY SHORT-TERM MEMORY MAY BE GONE, BUT I'M CURSED WITH LONG-TERM MEMORY. I ACTU-
ALLY REMEMBER THE DEVIL AND DANIEL MOUSE, ROCK & RULE (IS IT FINISHED YET?), AND EVEN
THE STUDIO AT QUEENS QUAY. IT HAS TRULY BEEN A DELIGHT BEING A FRIEND AND COLLEAGUE
OF MICHAEL, PATRICK, CLIVE, AND THE REST OF THE NELVANA GANG ALL THESE YEARS. THEY
HAVE NEVER LOST THEIR ENTHUSIASM AND HAVE NEVER STOPPED CARING ABOUT QUALITY.
DEBORAH BERNSTEIN, EXECUTIVE DIRECTOR, TV ARTS & ENTERTAINMENT, CBC TV

WHY IS NELVANA SUCCESSFUL? BECAUSE THE THREE PARTNERS COMPLEMENT EACH OTHER.
BECAUSE THEY ARE CRAZY. AND BECAUSE THEY HAVE ADJUSTED TO MEET THE GLOBAL MARKET
OPPORTUNITY.
JAMIE KELLNER, CHAIRMAN AND CEO, TURNER BROADCASTING

THE NELVANA STORY IS ABOUT THREE IDEALISTIC, CREATIVE, AND OCCASIONALLY CONFLICTED
HIPPIES WHO TURNED INTO THREE SAVVY ENTREPRENEURS. ALONG THE WAY, THEY DID IT ALL,
SAW IT ALL, REINVENTED THEMSELVES, THEIR COMPANY, AND THEIR RELATIONSHIP COUNTLESS
TIMES AND SURVIVED! IN A SENSE, IT'S A METAPHOR FOR THE EVOLUTION OF THE CANADIAN
TELEVISION PRODUCTION INDUSTRY... AND THE GOOD NEWS IS THAT THE BOYS ARE STILL AT IT,
GOING STRONG.
IVAN FECAN, CEO, BELL GLOBEMEDIA AND CTV INC.

IN THE WORDS OF RUPERT BROOKE, "I AM A PART OF ALL THAT I HAVE MET." WE CONSIDER
OURSELVES FORTUNATE TO BE ASSOCIATED WITH NELVANA.
MICKEY AND BETTY PARASKEVAS, CREATORS OF MAGGIE AND THE FEROCIOUS BEAST

CHAPTER 1 THE 1970s

Patrick Loubert sat bolt upright in bed. He glanced at the clock on the bedside table. It was 3 a.m. on a cold winter night on Toronto Island, and yet the lake, visible through the curtainless window, was bright as day. Two rings of lights were blinking on and off, high in the December sky.

Loubert threw on some clothes, grabbed his binoculars, and raced to the shore. McGonnigle, his German shepherd, ran at his side in a frenzy of excitement. "I could see very, very clearly," he recalls. "There were two rings of lights blinking on and off, about 10 miles from shore and seven miles up. They were rotating. One set of lights, and another above it."

Loubert wasn't the only one who saw strange lights that December night in 1975. He was among 180 people who phoned a UFO hotline to report unidentified flying objects over Lake Ontario.

The objects remained unidentified but they had a major impact on a fledgling film studio called Nelvana. Loubert was one of three filmmakers who had founded Nelvana four years previously, and the lights gave him an idea. Christmas was coming. What if the three wise men reappeared, arriving in a spaceship that lit up the sky?

The result of Loubert's inspiration was *Cosmic Christmas,* a half-hour animated television show that brought the story of the three wise men into the space age. *Cosmic Christmas* was a crucial turning point in the history of Nelvana because it marked the beginning of a journey that would take the company into the international big leagues of animated film production. The Christmas special was broadcast across the U.S. and Canada in 1977 and has since been seen in a total of 85 countries.

Until then, Loubert and his partners, Michael Hirsh and Clive Smith, had produced nothing remotely as ambitious. The CBC had given them some work making four-minute "fillers" to be aired when a regular program didn't quite fill an entire hour. And they had made a few short films combining live action and animation—"very, very silly" films as Clive Smith recalls them, such as *Zounds of Music,* the story of a musical note that ventures out into the busy streets of Toronto.

Hirsh, Loubert, and Smith had talent but no money and little experience. All they knew was that they wanted to build a film studio, an audacious project at a time when there was no such thing as a Canadian film studio. They were aspiring filmmakers, not businessmen, and they had no business plan. Ironically,

(RIGHT) MICHAEL HIRSH, PATRICK LOUBERT, AND CLIVE SMITH DISCUSS COSMIC CHRISTMAS WITH DESIGNER-ANIMATOR FRANK NISSEN (FOREGROUND). (BELOW) AN EARLY SKETCH OF PETER AND LUCY, CHARACTERS IN COSMIC CHRISTMAS. ART: FRANK NISSEN.

gling studio had done to that point, *Cosmic Christmas* was a Nelvana property that would become part of a valuable library of shows that can be shown over and over again to each new generation of kids.

In 2001, as Nelvana celebrates its 30th anniversary, it is the largest animation producer outside the U.S., providing work for 600 employees and thousands of freelancers. It has offices in six countries. As of 2001, it has 23 different series on the air and its productions are seen in 180 countries. In the U.S., Nelvana has more new shows on TV than Warner Brothers, creator of Bugs Bunny. It also has more new shows on U.S. TV than the Walt Disney Company, whose co-founder, Roy Disney, once owned a summer house on Toronto Island just steps from Loubert's. In fact, this Canadian company has more new shows on American television than those two American giants of animation combined. Nelvana, in short, has succeeded far beyond the expectations of anyone, including its founders.

Nelvana's success is the story of three young men starting small and becoming big and remaining partners for 30 years. It's also the story of hundreds of talented people, from both the creative and business sides, finding what it takes to win in an intense-

Cosmic Christmas, although they did not realize it back then, not even when the show became an international success, incarnated all the elements of the business plan that many years later would catapult their company into the big time.

Cosmic Christmas was the first Nelvana production that was entirely animated. It was the first produced for the U.S., taking advantage of the fact that the world's largest market for entertainment is next door and speaks the same language. And, unlike most of the small contract jobs the strug-

ly competitive industry. Finally, it's the story of how a small company specializing in animation led the way as Canada, starting from nothing 30 years ago, grew into the second largest exporter of television programs in the world.

Success has not erased Michael Hirsh's vivid memories of his early attempts to sell Nelvana's shows in the U.S.: "People would laugh at us because we were from Canada. I mean really laugh. You'd have to go through five minutes of jokes about being from Canada. They couldn't believe a studio in Canada had actually produced something. They thought it was a joke."

Nobody's laughing now—nobody except millions of kids enjoying the humour in the many Nelvana programs broadcast in dozens of languages on millions of television screens in every nook and cranny of the globe.

Michael Hirsh was born in Belgium. In 1951, at the age of three, he moved with his parents to Canada. Then, in 1961, the family moved again, this time to New York City, where the 13-year-old Hirsh enrolled in the Bronx High School of Science and began his career as a filmmaker. "I went to screenings of U.S. under-

(LEFT) ROUGH LAYOUT FOR A SCENE IN COSMIC CHRISTMAS.
(BELOW) DUCK DESIGN FOR EARLY CBC SHORT. ART: CLIVE SMITH.

ground films and became enamoured of independent filmmaking," he recalls. "I got an 8 mm camera and started making films, and I went to the local showcases in Manhattan for independent films."

The perpetual optimism that would later help him guide Nelvana through difficult times was already apparent. "I had an inability to distinguish between the junk I was doing and what people who had been working in film for years were generating. So I thought my early experimental films were on par with other experimental filmmakers." They weren't, of

course. In fact, the films of Hirsh's Bronx period were so forgettable that he has forgotten them himself.

Patrick Loubert had finished high school and was hitchhiking around Europe in 1967 with a cousin and her friend when something happened that would inspire his ambition to become a filmmaker. On a highway in the south of Italy, a large Mercedes pulled over to the side of the road and the driver told them to hop in. His name

(RIGHT) STUDIO PHOTOGRAPH TAKEN OUT-
SIDE THE TERMINAL WAREHOUSE BUILDING
ON QUEENS QUAY DURING PRODUCTION OF
ROCK & RULE, 1979. (BELOW) A PAGE FROM
SMITH'S SKETCHBOOK DEPICTING CHARAC-
TERS FOR NELVANA'S EARLY SHORTS.

THAT'S NICE YOU
OLD FART

was Gillo Pontecorvo and he was a movie director scouting for locations. "I had never heard of him," Loubert recalls. "He was a bit disappointed to learn that none of the three of us had seen any of his films and didn't know who he was."

When Loubert got back to Toronto, he enrolled at York University, where he attended a screening of Pontecorvo's masterpiece, *Battle of Algiers*, an account of the Algerian uprising against the French that was so realistic many viewers took it for a documentary. "After I saw it, I became interested in making films," says Loubert. "I bought myself a 16 mm Bolex movie camera at a pawn shop and started doing some of my own shooting around campus."

By then, Hirsh had also returned to Toronto, as a student at the Glendon College campus of York University. Hirsh and another student, Jack Christie, were making a movie they called *The Assassination Generation*, inspired by the assassinations during the 1960s of the Kennedy brothers and Martin Luther King.

Christie, now a Vancouver writer and broadcaster, recalls that Hirsh was "very interested in animation. The type of animation employed in *The Assassination Generation* is now fairly standard with the development of digital animation, but then it was very laborious. We had a split screen and two different story ideas running at the same time. For example, you have a string of pearls around a woman's neck and inside each pearl there's a little piece of animation."

While they were making *The Assassination Generation*, Hirsh and Christie met Loubert, who became a valuable part of their team. He was the only one of the three who owned a car. Loubert did some of the camera work on the movie, which would eventually be incorporated into a larger film called *Voulez-Vous Coucher Avec God?* Christie watched this film in 2000 for the first time in many years and says he was "surprised at how well it stood up. Not only does it have split screen cel animation but also elements of pixillation and claymation." (Pixillation, a style associated with the great Canadian animator Norman McLaren, uses live subjects filmed in various fixed poses. Claymation uses Plasticine figures that are changed in small ways to portray action.)

Because of a permanent money shortage, it took many years to complete *Voulez-Vous*, which finally had its debut at the 1972 Toronto Film Festival. In the meantime, Hirsh and Loubert had collaborated on a film based on "Rappaccini's Daughter," a story by Nathaniel Hawthorne. It was called *Rappapussy's Daughter* because, Loubert explains, "it was a send-up of the puritan sex ethic."

At one point, they got into trouble with the university because they had sent some bills to the York University film studies department, a department that did not then exist. "We were trying to get them [the university] to offer a film course," says Loubert. Hirsh and Loubert also staged mixed-media events featuring film and poetry readings. At one such event, they passed off a homeless man they had met on a Toronto street as the beat poet William Burroughs. The man read some of Burroughs's poetry and answered questions from an audience that was thrilled to be in the presence of so famous an author.

In 1967, Hirsh caught the attention of Mary Lou Stuerm, who had been recruited from the University of Michigan the year before to head the theatre department at York University. She had the task of organizing a four-day arts festival to commemorate Canada's centennial. "I wanted to have films running throughout the weekend. There were students at York doing their own short films,

using their friends as actors. It was similar to the underground film movement at the University of Michigan. Michael was part of that at York. I saw some of his work and asked if he would allow his films to be played as backgrounds at Burton Auditorium all through the weekend. Some of them were really odd. They were what we would now look on as 'art films.'"

That arts festival was most memorable for the concert debut of a poet named Leonard Cohen, but Stuerm says the experimental films "pulled that weekend together. Michael was really excited by film. It was an adventure for him."

In the late 1960s, Hirsh and Loubert began to look for paying work. They found it with the Toronto branch of a U.S.-based company, Cineplast, which specialized in Plasticine animation. Cineplast had a contract from the Jim Henson Company to do animated segments on letters of the alphabet for a new educational children's TV show called *Sesame Street*. Hirsh and Loubert did three letters—E, S, and U. Most of Cineplast's work was commercials, and Hirsh and Loubert failed in their attempt to have the company branch out into Canadian jobs instead of only U.S. subcontracts. "Michael quit, and I got fired" is Loubert's uncertain recol-

WOW! THREE MORE SHOVELS AND POP SAYS I CAN READ MY COMICS.

COMIC ART TRADITIONS IN CANADA, 1941–45. WOMEN LES GRANDS COURANTS DE LA BANDE ILLUSTRÉE AU CANADA

The National Gallery of Canada, Ottawa, 1972-73
Galerie nationale du Canada, Ottawa, 1972-1973

lection. "Or we both got fired. After that, we decided that we were going to start a company based on what, I have no idea. A lot of misplaced confidence."

Hirsh, Loubert, Christie, and another filmmaker, Peter Dewdney, joined forces in a partnership they called Laff Arts. They decided they needed business cards, so Hirsh, trying to track down an artist he knew, phoned Carole Pope, then an animation painter, now a well-known singer. She said the artist he had in mind had left town but recommended a recently arrived Englishman named Clive Smith.

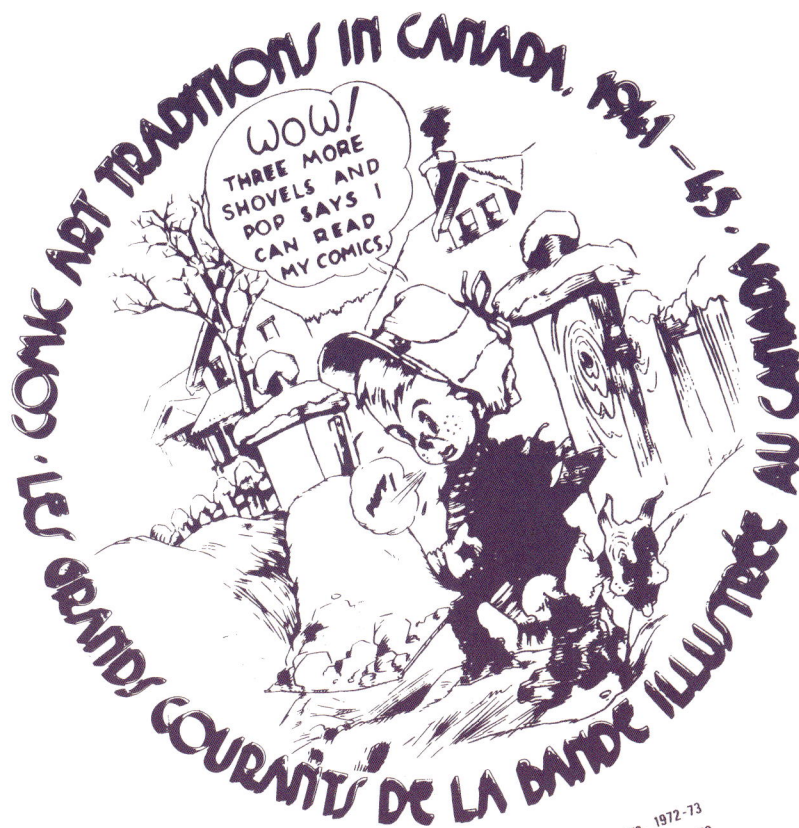

(OPPOSITE PAGE) THE EASTER BUNNY IS TOASTED IN NELVANA'S EASTER FEVER, DIRECTED BY KEN STEPHENSON AND RELEASED IN 1980. CHARACTERS WERE VOICED BY CATHERINE O'HARA, CHRIS WIGGINS, GARRET MORRIS, AND MAURICE LAMARSH.
(LEFT) THE TOURING EXHIBITION OF THE GREAT CANADIAN COMIC BOOK ART.
(BELOW) A LAUGH-A-LOTION, FROM INTERGALACTIC THANKSGIVING, 1975.

NELVANA OF THE NORTHERN LIGHTS

Best Wishes from Nelvana

Canadä

Smith, the son of a milkman, had grown up in a one-room flat in Willesden, in northern London. His earliest memories are of drawing things and making things. "There used to be these things on the back of Weetabix packages called Weetabix Workshop—a series of automobiles or buildings. You'd cut them out and construct them. I used to make up my own if I could get the cardboard. A nice fresh piece of cardboard was such a treasured thing, especially if it was white on one side. I was more thrilled by having that than my son is today by a new video game."

At the age of 15, Smith enrolled in the Ealing School of Art, where, in his second year, he came under the influence of a teacher named Roy Ascott. "He was a fan of Bauhaus, talked about cybernetic machines," Smith recalls. "It was unbelievably exciting to us, having done a year of charcoal drawings taught by old fuddy-duddies who were just following a routine. The first day, Roy said, 'You know nothing about anything. Nothing about colour, shape, form, or line. We have to go back to basics. The dot. When you understand the dot, then we'll move on to the line.'"

Smith drew a dot three feet wide and 50 yards long, which he rolled out down the corridor. Other students did three-dimensional dots, still others hanging dots. "He [Ascott] started a thought process, started people doing ingenious and inventive things," says Smith.

While at Ealing, the seeds of Smith's future career were planted when the film club showed *The Little Island*, an animated film by Richard Williams. "It blew me away," he recalls. "I didn't pursue animation at the time but I knew that was something I would like to do."

After acquiring a diploma in design, Smith jumped enthusiastically into the artistic life of London in the swinging 1960s. He played piano in several bands and painted pop art on King's Road storefronts. One day, in search of work, he wandered into the offices of a company called Group Two, which was producing an animated television series on the Beatles and another based on the Lone Ranger.

He immediately felt at home amid the paint and drawings and cameras and was thrilled to discover that people could actually make a living by drawing. "I talked myself into a job working on *The Lone Ranger* as an in-betweener. I spent my first day painting cels." (A cel is a transparent sheet of celluloid on which an animation drawing is painted. "In-betweening" is work typically assigned to novice animators; an in-betweener draws the less important frames between one key scene and the next.)

Smith stayed at Group Two for two years, until the company went out of business. Then he went back to playing piano in rock bands and did some freelance in-betweening on the Beatles movie *Yellow Submarine.* He tried for full-time work at several studios but was turned down for being too inexperienced. Then, in 1967, a Canadian named Vladimir Goetzleman arrived in London on the hunt for animators to work at Al Guest Animation, then Canada's largest animation studio. Smith didn't want to leave London but he did want to work. Goetzleman was offering free airfare and a salary of $110 a week, which was vastly more than the three pounds, 10 shillings per week Smith had earned at his previous full-time job.

"I came to Canada for one year," Smith recalls. "I gave my record collection to somebody in England, I gave him my piano, books, animation equipment and said, 'Look after this. I'll be back in a year.' Well, the year went by in about 15 minutes. I was just getting into things."

He soon discovered that the job he had been recruited for—animating a series called *Rocket Robin Hood*—was not to his liking. "It was a pretty awful show, so I worked on commercials instead." As had the previous animation company Smith worked for,

Al Guest Animation went out of business and Smith became a freelancer again, doing animation and illustration.

That's when Michael Hirsh hired him to design a business card for Laff Arts. The front of the card Smith designed showed an overweight man in a suit. When flipped open, his pants had dropped to his feet, his shirt was off, and he was wearing only a T-shirt and boxer shorts. The card was clever and funny but it did nothing for Laff Arts' business. Even the name "Laff Arts" was too flippant for the ad agencies Hirsh and Loubert were approaching to try to get work doing commercials. Add to this that Hirsh's one suit, purchased at the Salvation Army, was a bit frayed at the edges and that he always wore soccer shoes with it (they were his only pair), and it's understandable why potential clients were dubious about Laff Arts.

Loubert recalls: "We sort of hacked around and took meetings and we really weren't getting anywhere. Then somebody said, 'Do you do animation?'

"I said, 'Of course we do animation—that's what we specialize in.'"

In fact, Hirsh and Loubert saw themselves as filmmakers, not animators, and were equally interested in live action. But when you're starting out, you look for needs to fill. "It was the equivalent of taking in laundry," Loubert says. "We did anything anybody wanted us to do."

They got work doing titles for Film Arts, a small Toronto editing service, and short Plasticine animation bits for the Ontario educational network. There was also a contract to write a 10-minute cartoon called *Super Joe*, about the National Football League star Joe Namath. Another job involved editing footage other filmmakers had shot about the Toronto Stock Exchange. And Hirsh and Loubert wrote and produced a CBC television show about the "Canadian whites," comic books produced in Canada during World War II. Meanwhile, Jack Christie, who had

been a partner in Laff Arts, got a grant to complete *Voulez-Vous Coucher Avec God*? He moved to Ottawa to work on the film at the studios of Crawley Films.

Laff Arts had a studio on Brant Street, a low-rent district at the edge of the city's business core. Another tenant there was Gerry Wills, a Toronto Island neighbour of Loubert's who had a one-man candle factory. "We were all a bunch of young hippies," recalls Wills, who today operates the cafeteria at the Nelvana office and studio complex on Atlantic Avenue in Toronto. "They made films,

I made candles. They had no money and neither did I, but I had candles."

Candles were a better business than films. Wills made multicoloured candles, then a novelty, and in the days before Christmas 1969, Loubert and Hirsh took to the streets of downtown Toronto to sell them. Neither knew much about business, and selling Wills's candles taught them a fundamental principle of economics: the law of supply and demand. "We started at $3 a candle," recalls Loubert, "and business was so good that we moved that up to $5. Nobody else had candles like these, and they were very

(RIGHT) LOUBERT AND HIRSH BROWSE THROUGH THE CANADIAN COMICS, THE SOURCE OF SEVERAL EARLY PROJECTS AND INSPIRATION FOR THE NAME OF THE FLEDGLING COMPANY, 1971.

easy to sell. So we moved the price up to three for $20. The day before Christmas, we had five candles left and we sold them for $20 each. We made about $400 in a few days, at a time when we had been making about 25 bucks a week. It was the most money we made all year."

But Hirsh and Loubert were determined to be in the film business, not the candle business. Clive Smith, who was enjoying success freelancing for advertising agencies and was not a partner in Laff Arts, had the same ambition. Hirsh and Loubert decided Laff Arts, which had been in business for all of a year, wasn't working. The three of them decided to incorporate a new company under a name that would be taken seriously. "There were people in ad agencies who liked us," recalls Hirsh. "They would say, 'I like your creativity, but I can't sell you to clients as Laff Arts. Maybe if this were New York or L.A., but not Toronto. Get a name that is neutral-sounding that could be anything but sounds nice.' Then we thought of Nelvana."

During World War II, there was little money available to import non-necessities, so the Canadian government banned, among other things, the import of comic books. Canadian entrepreneurs quickly stepped in to fill the void and created Canadian comic books with Canadian heroes—Johnny Canuck, Dixon of the Mounted, Derek of Bras d'Or, and Nelvana of the Northern Lights. Most of them were printed in black and white, which is why they later became known among collectors as the "Canadian whites."

The indigenous comic book industry faded away after the war ended, and copies of the Canadian whites became scarce. John Ezrin, one of the businessmen who had created the industry, kept a stash of them, along

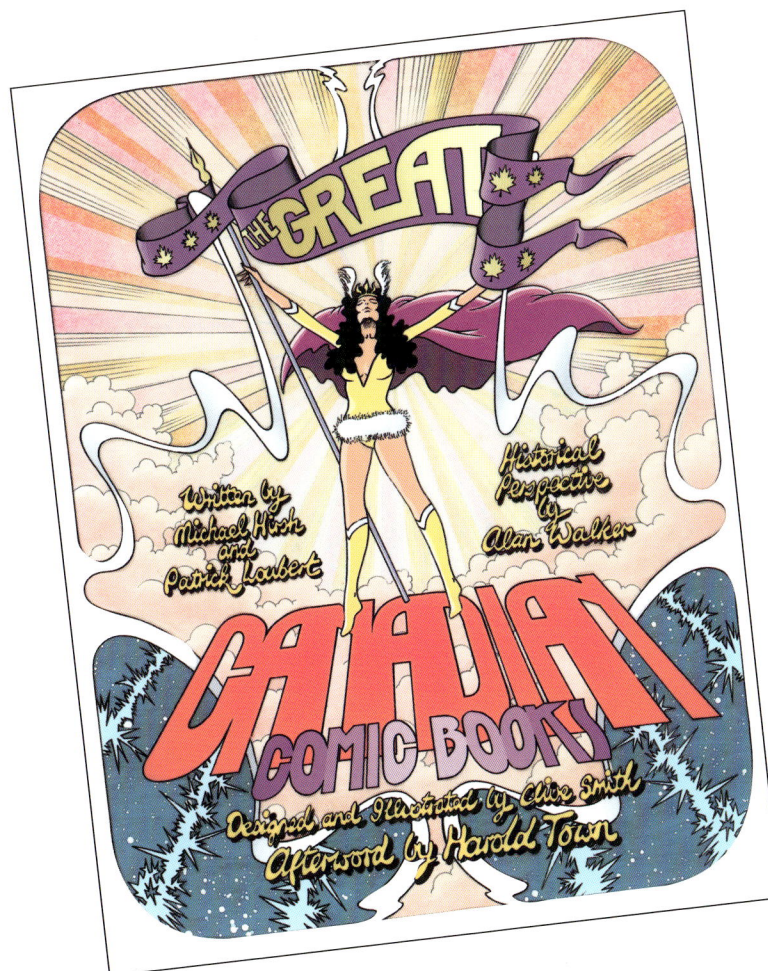

THE GREAT CANADIAN COMIC BOOKS

Written by Michael Hirsh and Patrick Loubert

Historical Perspective by Alan Walker

Designed and Illustrated by Clive Smith

Afterword by Harold Town

(LEFT) THE COVER OF NELVANA'S FIRST BOOK, A COMPILATION AND HISTORICAL REVIEW OF THE "CANADIAN WHITES." ART: CLIVE SMITH. (BELOW) AN ILLUSTRATION FROM A CHAPTER HEADING IN THE GREAT CANADIAN COMIC BOOKS. ART: CLIVE SMITH.

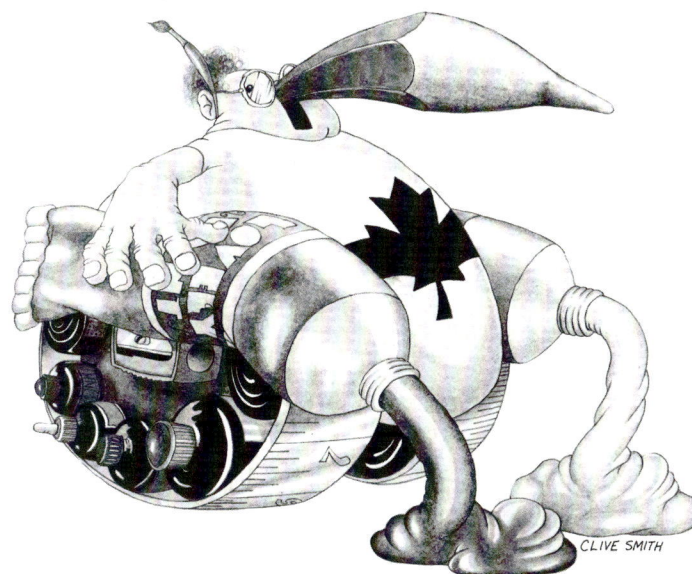

CLIVE SMITH

with some of the original art, photo negatives, and printing plates. By 1970, Ezrin was looking to unload this important chunk of Canadian literary history but he wanted to find a good home for it.

Ezrin met two young men who seemed to fit the bill. "I thought they could do something with the comics," he told writer Alan Walker in 1971. "They had done a lot of research into them, they liked them—and mostly they struck me as doers. I've always been a doer myself. All in all, I decided that these boys deserved the comics, and everything that went with them."

So he sold them to Michael Hirsh and Patrick Loubert, who proceeded to mount a travelling show on the comics for the National Gallery of Canada. They tracked down and interviewed all of the original artists they could find and, in addition to the CBC program, they produced a book, *The Great Canadian Comic Books*, that included reproductions of episodes of the leading titles. Loubert and Hirsh wrote the text, and Clive Smith designed and illustrated it. Hirsh and Loubert later sold the original artwork and two sets of the comics to the Museum of Man in Ottawa.

The first story in the book is an episode dating from the 1940s of *Nelvana of the Northern Lights*, star-ring Nelvana, daughter of Koliak, king of the northern lights. The beautiful and fearless Nelvana, a creation of artist Adrian Dingle, could become invisible when threatened with danger by absorbing herself into Koliak's "powerful ray."

By 1971, almost no one remembered Nelvana (although years later she would adorn a Canadian stamp), but that didn't matter when it came time to choose a name for the new film company. Hirsh explains: "It was a great-sounding name, it didn't mean anything, it had Canadian identifica-

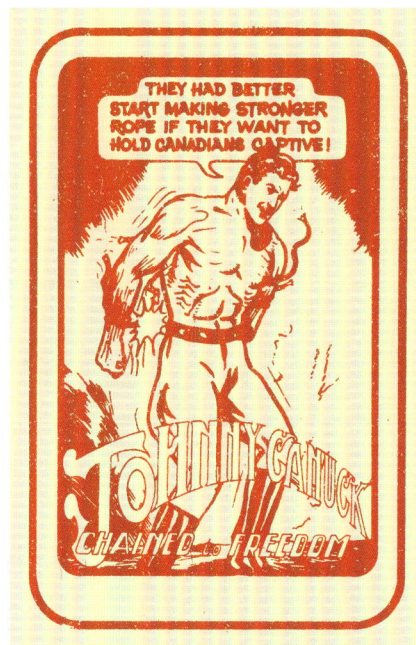

THEY HAD BETTER START MAKING STRONGER ROPE IF THEY WANT TO HOLD CANADIANS CAPTIVE!

JOHNNY CANUCK CHAINED to FREEDOM

(OPPOSITE PAGE) FROM ROMIE-O AND JULIE-8. (LEFT) A COMMEMORATIVE STAMP FOR THE GREAT CANADIAN COMIC BOOKS WAS ISSUED BY CANADA POST. (BELOW) SMITH AD-LIBBED THIS CUTOUT MODEL OF JOHNNY CANUCK FOR THE SOUVENIR ARTPACK THAT ACCOMPANIED THE TRAVELLING THE GREAT CANADIAN COMIC BOOKS EXHIBITION.

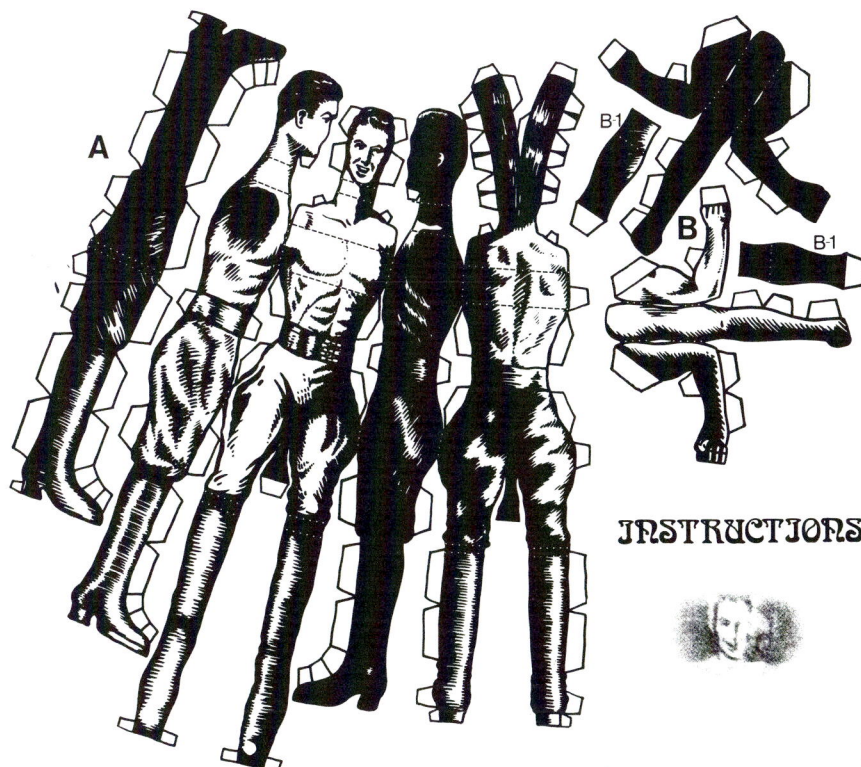

A

B1

B

B-1

INSTRUCTIONS

(RIGHT) SMITH AS MR. PENCIL.
(BELOW) MR. PENCIL. ART: CLIVE SMITH.

to service the needs of U.S. producers who had discovered that they could make movies and TV shows more cheaply in Canada than at home. But nobody had yet succeeded in doing what Hirsh, Loubert, and Smith were proposing to do—establish a for-profit Canadian movie company.

It was natural that the fledgling company would look to the CBC as a source of business. The CBC needed fillers—four-minute films to air when a program didn't quite run to the end of an hour. The filler genre, as developed by the CBC, was more difficult than it sounds. A filler had to be interesting enough to hold the viewer's attention until the next scheduled program came on. But—and this was the hard part—it couldn't be too interesting or the viewer would be upset if it was cut off in the middle. That happened when the network didn't need to fill four minutes. Often, it needed to fill only two or three minutes.

When the Nelvana trio began making fillers, they saw it as an opportunity to show how creative they were. "We wrote all these elaborate plots and stories," Clive Smith recalls. In one of them, Smith played a man who walked around the city and kept meeting himself as an old man, a part also played by Smith, made up to look old. But Rena Krawagna, a CBC execu-

tion because of the comic book, it had history—and we owned it."

The only people who thought starting Nelvana was a good idea were Hirsh, Loubert, and Smith. Don Haig, who ran Film Arts, asked Hirsh why he wanted to start a film company.

Hirsh said, "We want to get into the industry."

Haig said, "There is no industry to get into."

That was only a slight exaggeration. In 1971, there was no independent film production industry in Canada. Apart from the films produced by the CBC and the National Film Board, the only domestic productions were the occasional movies financed by Telefilm Canada, another government agency. Private production companies made television commercials. An industry was developing

tive who was a buyer of fillers and children's programs, was not impressed. "No," she would say, "that's not a filler."

They eventually figured out that the ideal filler showed a process such as pottery or candle making that was interesting but not so interesting that the viewer needed to see how it ended. "Fillers kept us alive in the early days," says Smith. "Rena would buy 10 fillers, and with what she would pay, we could produce a short film and make the fillers with what was left over."

Overpaying for the fillers was a deliberate strategy used by Krawagna, who had a small budget for children's programs and a big budget for fillers. She would buy the shows Nelvana made with its excess filler money for CBC's children's department. In this way, Nelvana was able to finance 10 films, each 15 minutes long, half animated and half live action. They called the series Small Star Cinema. Hirsh wrote and directed one film called *Mr. Pencil Draws the Line*, starring Smith as a pencil. Smith, who has a photo of himself dressed as a pencil hanging on his office wall, still remembers walking across Nathan Phillips Square in downtown Toronto in his costume while being harassed by a citizen who, for unknown rea-

sons, was outraged by the spectacle. He chased after Smith, angrily shouting over and over again, "Who are you? I'm talking to you."

The culmination of Smith's acting career was another Small Star film, *Mr. Rubbish and the Conductor's Guided Tour of the City*. The idea had come to him one Halloween when he had nothing to wear to a party and so he had grabbed a green garbage bag and wore that. The movie was a re-enactment, with Smith clothed in a garbage bag, tights, and frogman slippers. He had green hair and a green painted face. Loubert made an appearance as the tour conductor, and Carole Pope, with whom Smith also performed in a band, was the narrator.

Zounds of Music, another memorable Small Star production, starred Gerry Wills, the former candle maker. The movie was an attempt to answer a question that had never been asked before: "Where does the music go when it leaves the radio?"

Loubert, the director, asked Wills, "Can you roller skate?"

Wills said, "No."

Loubert said, "Give it a try and

you can keep the roller skates. You also get lunch."

Because *Zounds of Music* was both the beginning and the end of his acting career, Wills remembers it well. "I was dressed up as a [music] note. The costume had big satin shorts full of Styrofoam. And this really tight top. Clive spray painted a silver note on my chest. I was so embarrassed.

"I escaped from this little music shop at Yonge and Dundas. I was to leap out of the doorway, across the sidewalk, and

NELVANA'S EARLY ANIMATION TECHNIQUES WERE LIMITED BY THE TOOLS. CUTOUTS WERE MANIPULATED ON A MAKESHIFT ANIMATION STAND USING A WIND-UP BOLEX.

across the street. That was the note escaping from the radio. There was just Patrick, the camera guy, and myself. No traffic control. It was my first time on roller skates. I just leaped out there. It looked like I was acting but I wasn't—I was just trying to survive getting across the street. I had no way to stop, and Patrick realized this. When I was about 25 feet away, he had to leap in front of me and catch me and throw me to the ground because he was afraid I was going to bowl over the camera, which was a rental. None of the cars looked like they were going to stop. It happened so fast they didn't have a chance. It was a miracle that I made it across the street."

After Wills had caught his breath, Loubert said, "I think we should do it again just to make sure that we got it right."

"You're kidding."

"No, let's do it again."

So they did it again, and Wills made it across the street a second time. "It [the filming] took two days, so I got two lunches," he recalls.

Along with Rena Krawagna of the CBC, a benefactor of Nelvana's early days was Don Haig. Both he and Krawagna were on the Ontario Arts Council, which gave grants to filmmakers, and were dedicated to encouraging young talent. "People would apply to make a film," Haig recalls. "She had a place to broadcast it, and I had editing facilities."

If Haig thought young filmmakers had talent, he would let them work at night at Film Arts at no cost, whether they were grant recipients or not. Among those who benefited from his largesse was Patricia Rozema, who went on to make the hit film *I Heard the Mermaids Singing.*

"I gave [the Nelvana trio] the

editing room and transferring facilities for sound," Haig recalls. "I kind of hovered around to make sure their films looked presentable, that there was colour and sound, because I knew the CBC would take them through Rena.

"I was really interested in the development of upcoming talent because they worked like hell and they had great ideas, and I think that's how the Nelvana boys struck me— they were very hard-working, starving to death, but there was a talent and an excitement. Clive is an artist. I was totally fascinated by his talent. It was just weird, off the wall. Michael was more of the businessperson, behind the creative scenes. He was the guy making the deals, even then. He would say, 'How can we do this?' It's hard to remember, but I'm sure I eventually got paid back for film stock after the films were sold to CBC. It was fun taking a chance with these guys."

Haig got them work doing high-contrast titles, consisting of white letters on a black background. This is work that is now done digitally, but in those days, titles were a labour-intensive process. "It was another thing we could do to stay alive," Loubert says. "Don was nice enough to keep us in business with hi-con titles, although there were a lot of

people who could do it better than we could. He's a real nice man."

How important was Haig to Nelvana's ability to stay in business during its early years? "The only way we survived was [by] doing the editing on the midnight shift, which he gave us for free," Hirsh says.

Another reason Nelvana survived was Loubert's Chargex card. One way issuers of credit cards can acquire customers is by sending unsolicited cards to students upon their graduation from university. Loubert, unlike Hirsh, had actually graduated from York and so, along with his diploma, he received a Chargex card (precursor of Visa) from the Canadian Imperial Bank of Commerce (CIBC). Loubert, Hirsh, and Smith used the card as a credit line for their infant film company.

One day, the three of them were lunching at an Italian restaurant on King Street in Toronto, celebrating because a potential client had agreed to meet with them. At the end of the meal, Loubert plunked the card down as payment. The waiter took it but did not return. After an unusual delay, the manager of the restaurant came to the table wielding a pair of scissors. He cut the card in two and presented it to Loubert on a tray. He said, "Your bank manager would like to speak with you."

Loubert went to see T.E. Osborne, manager of the CIBC branch at Rochdale College on Bloor Street, near the University of Toronto.

Osborne said, "You haven't made a payment on your Chargex since you got it."

"I never asked for that card," Loubert explained.

The credit limit on the card was $5,000, but Nelvana had been able to pile up $7,500 worth of debt on it.

Osborne said, "You're going to have to pay this money back."

Loubert said he wasn't sure how he could do that.

Osborne asked, "What are you guys anyway?"

"We're a film company."

"Oh, really? What kind of film company?"

Loubert explained about the films and fillers and animated titles that Nelvana was making. His story must have been impressive because the bank manager decided the Nelvana loan was an asset he would like to have on his own branch's books.

"What I'm going to do," he said, "is give you $7,500, and you're going to give it back to me to pay off the card and then you will have a loan at this branch."

Loubert asked, "Why don't you give us $15,000 and we will pay Chargex and keep the other $7,500?"

Osborne agreed, and Nelvana had its first legitimate credit line.

Few businesses can survive without a credit line, but for a film production company, it is absolutely essential. Actors, animators, directors,

and all the other workers have to be paid immediately, while the buyers of the finished programs, even the most solvent ones, are notoriously slow to pay.

Getting the loan from the CIBC Rochdale branch was a stroke of luck made possible, Michael Hirsh believes, because the bank manager did not understand the film business. "Either that or he was a really helpful guy. He only asked what our receivables were. He never asked what our payables were." At the time, Nelvana's system for dealing with payables was as follows: A stack of invoices was kept in a shoebox, with the oldest invoices on the bottom and the most recent on top. On those occasions when there was money in the company's bank account, one of the partners would pull out the bottom invoice. If it was for less than what was in the bank, it got paid; if it was for more, it went to the top of the pile.

Rochdale College, a headquarters for the radical youth movement of the 1960s and 1970s, was a hive of creative and other business activity, and the bank branch there was a busy one. "That branch was making a ton of money," says Hirsh, "so the manager had more flexibility than he otherwise would have."

The relationship was often a rocky

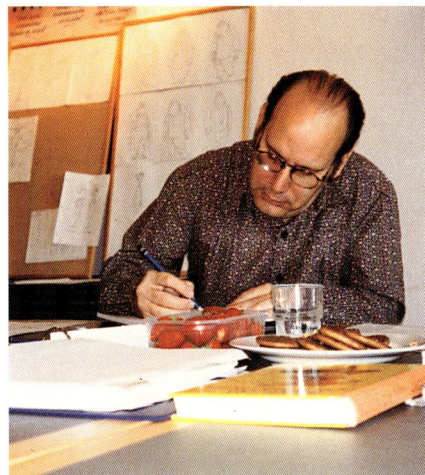

(OPPOSITE PAGE) FROM THE DEVIL AND DANIEL MOUSE. (ABOVE LEFT) ART: DAVE THRASHER. (LEFT) FRANK NISSEN WORKED ON MANY NELVANA FILMS. SHOWN HERE AT WORK IN STOCKHOLM.

one. The bank was not satisfied that the company's financial affairs were in order and put pressure on the partners to obtain the services of an accountant. Finally, they gathered their shoeboxes full of papers and turned them over to an accountant who lived in Rochdale and who handled the books of several other creative and unconventional enterprises. They did not know that the accountant was a heavy drug user who had recently suffered a nervous breakdown.

The bank manager who succeeded Osborne wanted to see Nelvana's books. For weeks, the accountant stalled. Finally, he could put it off no longer. He showed up at the bank for a meeting with the manager, dressed as a wizard, with a robe down to his ankles and a conical hat. In his hand was a long staff. He entered the manager's office and plunked down a $2 bill on the desk.

The accountant demanded, "What is that?"

The manager said, "It's a $2 bill."

"No it isn't!" shrieked the accountant. "It's just a piece of paper."

He then struck the manager several times with his staff before being subdued by bank employees. No charges were laid, but the CIBC was not amused, especially since the manager had just come back from a leave

occasioned by a nervous breakdown of his own. The bank ordered Nelvana to obtain the services of a less excitable accountant and the company complied.

This incident, which took place in 1974, was the low point in Nelvana's relationships with its lenders, although there would be other turbulent times ahead. By then, however, the company had more projects under way and was starting to enjoy its first real success. It got its biggest contract ever, from the federal Department of Energy, to do an educational program —half live action, half animation—on energy management. The show was entitled *Energy Management for the*

Future—not the most exciting stuff, but it gave Smith the opportunity to assemble a team of Sheridan graduates to help him animate characters he called energy servants. In 1975, Loubert completed *125 Rooms of Comfort*, a live action feature he wrote and directed, with Jackie Burroughs in the starring role. The movie, produced by Don Haig's company, Film Arts, was shot in St. Thomas, west of Toronto, on a budget of about $125,000.

During this period, Nelvana had a small studio on King Street. The company car was Smith's old Eaton's van, with the skull of a bull attached to the front bumper. The division of labour

that continues to this day was already becoming evident. Hirsh was beginning to specialize in sales, Loubert in production, and Smith—the only one who knew how to draw—in creating programs. In the King Street studio, an important part of Smith's domain was the second toilet. This was where he had set up his camera room, the place he could film animated drawings. He turned the water off, installed a light inside the toilet bowl, and put a table over the toilet. He would design animated sequences, do the backgrounds and animations, place them on the illuminated table over the toilet, and then shoot them with a wind-up camera placed atop a pole. The camera lacked a zoom lens, so zooming was done by placing a pile of books beneath the artwork.

One day, a young man named Woody Yocum stopped Smith on the street and asked for work. Nelvana couldn't afford to hire anyone, but Yocum kept hanging around the studio. Eventually Smith hired him on a freelance basis to work on a project. Yocum became Nelvana's first employee. The second was Dave Thrasher, a graduate of the animation program at Toronto's Sheridan College, who came to work on the animated sequences of a half-hour show, half animated and half live action, called *Christmas Two*

Step. Produced in 1975 for the English and French CBC networks, it was about a young girl who wants to be the lead dancer in a Christmas pageant.

Nelvana has never been purely an animation company. But by 1975 it was becoming evident that there were good reasons for continuing to specialize in animation. For one thing, Nelvana was good at it, as the warm reception to the animated sequences in *Christmas Two Step* showed. For another, there was less competition in that field. Hardly anyone was producing commercial animation in the 1970s, and the conventional wisdom in the entertainment industry was that it was a dying art form. Hirsh, Loubert, and Smith did not share that opinion. A third, and totally fortuitous,

(LEFT) PETER DEWDNEY AND HIRSH AT THE KING STREET STUDIO, CIRCA 1970. IN THE BACKGROUND, A GIANT STAND-UP JOHNNY CANUCK. (BELOW) ANIMATOR DAVE THRASHER'S RENDERING OF THE SINGING, DANCING GRANDFATHER CLOCK IN NELVANA'S 1972 SPECIAL CHRISTMAS TWO STEP.

(RIGHT) THE LAND OF THE LAUGH-A-LOTIONS, INTERGALACTIC THANKSGIVING. (BELOW) SKETCH: CLIVE SMITH.

circumstance was the presence in the Toronto labour market of a growing number of highly skilled animators, the products of the recently launched animation program at Sheridan College.

Hirsh spotted what he believed was a "classic capitalist situation;" namely, the combination of unfilled demand for animated children's shows and the presence, because of the Sheridan program, of people who could create them. It was while Hirsh, Loubert, and Smith were mulling this over that Loubert was roused from his slumber on a cold winter night by the bizarre rotating lights over Toronto's harbour, prompting his idea about three wise men from outer space. The idea had arrived at just the right time.

Other filmmakers warned Smith that an animated project as big as *Cosmic Christmas* couldn't be done in Toronto. He set out to prove them wrong and recruited a talented team of 13 animators, including Dave Thrasher, Charles Bonafacio, John Halfpenny, and Frank Nissen. Some of these artists would later go on to work for Disney and other U.S.-based studios. Hirsh and Loubert, meanwhile, found backers to finance the show and drew up a budget of $275,000. The CBC bought it in advance, but that wasn't enough to make back the costs. Hirsh decided that *Cosmic*

Christmas would be Nelvana's entry into the world outside Canada.

Hirsh thought he would either sell *Cosmic Christmas* to one of the U.S. networks or to an advertising agency that would place it on a network. So he engaged a consultant who organized meetings with buyers from networks and advertising agencies. "I started going down to pitch the project," Hirsh recalls. Because the show wasn't yet made, all he was able to show the buyers were some colour pictures of the characters, a script, and a bit of animation.

First he had to sit through the jokes about Canada. Then he had to listen to complaints that the show lacked a big name—Sylvia Tyson, the best-known voice on *Cosmic Christmas*, was a big name in Canada but not in the U.S. Otherwise, Hirsh's pitch was well received. "People liked it because it was an original idea and there hadn't been a new Christmas project in a few years. But there was uncertainty about buying a show from us because there was no guarantee that we would deliver."

Jeffrey Kirsch, the financier behind *Cosmic Christmas*, suggested that Hirsh meet with Jamie Kellner, a young executive with Viacom, a syndication company. Viacom had previously been part of CBS but had recent-

(LEFT) JAN MOUSE SIGNS A DEAL WITH B.L. ZEEBUB'S MANAGER WEEZ WEEZEL IN THE DEVIL AND DANIEL MOUSE. CHARACTER ART: ROBIN BUDD. BACKGROUND ART: LOUIS KRAWAGNA.
(BELOW) ART: CLIVE SMITH

ly been spun off because the U.S. government, as part of its policy of reducing the power of the major networks, had required them to get rid of their syndication arms. Hirsh didn't think Nelvana could recover the cost of making *Cosmic Christmas* by syndicating it. However, he was interested in having Viacom's international arm distribute the show outside North America, and so he set up a meeting to pitch the project to Kellner.

Kellner immediately offered to buy it. Hirsh said, "No. NBC and ABC are interested, and I would rather sell it to one of them."

Kellner said, "That's great, but they'll lead you along, and in the end

they may not buy, in which case you'll have nothing. I'll syndicate this show and you'll get 97 per cent coverage of the U.S., which is the same as you get from a network. I'll get 7 p.m. or 7:30 p.m. and we'll get a big rating, and you'll make lots of money."

Kellner's point was that U.S. regulations had established 7 p.m. to 8 p.m. as a family viewing hour that was not available to the networks, so even network affiliates were looking to buy independent productions for that time slot. Kellner, who had the best Canada jokes of anyone Hirsh met on his sales foray, was persuasive. Nelvana sold Viacom the U.S. syndication rights to

Cosmic Christmas as well as the rights for other foreign countries.

It had taken Hirsh nine months to get a distribution deal for *Cosmic Christmas*, but it was worth the effort. The show got a 14.1 national rating when it showed across the U.S. in December 1977. At the time, it was one of the highest ratings ever for a syndicated show. Viacom also sold the show around the world. And Nelvana made back its costs.

Kellner was so enthusiastic about *Cosmic Christmas* that he tried to persuade Nelvana to do a series based on the three spacemen. Hirsh was for it, but Loubert and Smith overruled him. It was, however, the beginning of an important relationship with Viacom, which syndicated five more Nelvana specials, each pegged to a major holiday. Kellner eventually became a member of the company's board of directors.

Just as *Cosmic Christmas* marked Nelvana's debut on the international stage, so it had a major impact on the company internally. Animation was, and still is, a labour-intensive industry, and the staff increased from a dozen people to about 70 during production. "*Cosmic Christmas* drew on all our creative resources and storytelling," says Smith. "It allowed us to develop the process of making a film.

(OPPOSITE PAGE) THE DEVIL IN THE FINALE OF THE DEVIL AND DANIEL MOUSE, 1978. (LEFT) SMITH WITH LOVIN' SPOONFUL'S JOHN SEBASTIAN, WRITER AND PRODUCER OF SONGS FOR THE DEVIL AND DANIEL MOUSE. (BELOW LEFT) DANIEL MOUSE.

We'd never done it before from story to broadcast. We broke it down into 40 different building blocks. Before, when I was doing something by myself, I would design, draw, paint, and try different methods using animation cels or putting a bit of colour in, see if it worked, try it as a cutout. That was the way I worked. But when you are working on a production with a number of people, it has to be regimented, it has to be very organized. All of a sudden, we had to create the process to make that happen. It was a totally different level of production."

Did the success of *Cosmic Christmas* convince Nelvana's partners

(RIGHT) R2-D2 AND C-3PO FROM NELVANA'S TELEVISION SERIES "DROIDS." DESIGNER: FRANK NISSEN. (BELOW) KING GUCCI, INTERGALACTIC THANKSGIVING.

that their future was to build one of the world's most important animation studios? Not really. "We had the vision of a film studio," says Loubert. "I never thought we would end up in animation, and the reason we ended up in animation was that it was the one thing the CBC couldn't do themselves."

Nelvana produced another special, *The Devil and Daniel Mouse*, in 1978 and two each in 1979 and 1980. The shows were critically well received and still form part of Nelvana's film library. They also marked the first

times Nelvana employed major stars: Phil Silvers voiced a role in *Take Me Up to the Ballgame* and Sid Ceasar did one in *Intergalactic Thanksgiving*.

Looking at them now, however, Hirsh detects an important flaw—they are overly influenced by the period, the 1970s, in which they were made. "We didn't make them as evergreen as we should have," he says. "They look a little dated now. We learned a lesson from that."

Several of the specials involved space travel, a theme that particularly fascinated Hirsh, with his Bronx High School of Science background. It was

also a theme that fascinated an American filmmaker named George Lucas, whose first *Star Wars* movie had come out a few months before *Cosmic Christmas*. The next major step in building Nelvana's credibility as an important player in the film industry would be its professional relationship with George Lucas.

Lucas had hired David Acomba, a Canadian producer, to direct a TV special called *The Star Wars Holiday Special* for Thanksgiving 1978. This was a business decision, sparked by the huge success of *Star Wars* and *Star Wars* merchandise and by Kenner Toys' need to keep the *Star Wars* characters in front of children until the sequel arrived on movie screens in 1980. The Thanksgiving special was live action, but Lucas wanted a 10-minute animated sequence in it that would introduce a new character named Boba Fett, who would also appear in the sequel.

Lucas and Acomba had both admired *Cosmic Christmas,* and in March, Hirsh got a call from Acomba asking if Nelvana would be interested in doing the animated sequence for the *Star Wars* special. Nelvana wasn't the choice of the TV network that was going to broadcast the show. Its executives would have preferred that Lucas give the job to Hanna Barbera or some other established U.S. animation house. But Lucas favoured Nelvana. "He himself operates out of the L.A. maelstrom, in Marin County in northern California," explains Hirsh. "He was a supporter of independent filmmakers and he wanted to break out of the factory mode. He had seen our show, liked it, and thought we could do something interesting for him."

To seal the deal, Hirsh travelled to California. He flew to San Francisco and drove to Lucas's headquarters in San Rafael. Lucas likes his privacy, and finding his studio was a bit like tracking down an address in Tokyo, where most of the streets are unnamed. Hirsh recalls: "The directions were along the lines of, 'Go to this shopping centre, and then phone us and we'll give you the next direction.'" He found Lucas eventually, and the director drove Hirsh to a nearby Taco Bell for lunch in his 10-year-old Camaro. "The bill was for a couple of dollars. I wasn't sure if I should be paying or not. There was a pause—and he picked up the tab."

Lucas must have been satisfied with Hirsh's pitch because Nelvana got the job. Smith and Frank Nissen, a talented animator who now works for Disney in Los Angeles, got to work turning Lucas's script into a story-board, mapping out each frame of the 10-minute segment. (A storyboard is a series of sketches that tell the story, as in a comic.) Lucas wanted them to emulate the visual style of Moebius, the pseudonym of French artist Jean Giraud, whose work has a fantastic, dreamlike quality.

"Frank and I worked on the storyboard day and night," Smith recalls. "It was George's script. We followed it fairly closely. We had to develop the character of Boba Fett. George had designed a costume and sent us footage of someone wearing it. We used that to design the character. Frank and I got it working really well, but there were a couple of places that didn't feel comfortable. We didn't have time to fix them. We thought we would deal with them when we got into production.

"I took it down to present it to George. I showed a film strip; there must have been about 600 frames. I presented them to a room full of strangers. It took two hours to get through this 10-minute segment. You could hear a pin drop in this room. I was getting no feedback at all. Finally, I got through the whole thing —and when I finished, there was huge applause."

In addition to the film strip, the storyboard was pinned up on the

SOME OF THE MANY VOICE AND MUSIC TALENTS FEATURED IN NELVANA'S TELEVISION SPECIALS. TOP TO BOTTOM: CATHERINE O'HARA; JOHN SEBASTIAN DIRECTS BACK-UP SINGERS; SMITH WITH SID CEASAR IN PARIS COMPLETING INTERGALACTIC THANKSGIVING; JOHN CELESTRI DIRECTS GARRET MORRIS IN A SCENE FROM EASTER FEVER.

(ABOVE) FROM EASTER FEVER. (RIGHT) MARY BERTOIA, NELVANA COLOURIST, PAINT SUPERVISOR, AND GRAPHIC ARTIST SINCE 1976.

walls. Lucas, who had said nothing, strode to the wall and went right to the two places in the sequence that had been bothering Smith and instructed him on how to fix them. "He just went right to those two shots, asked for the changes, and went on with his work," says Hirsh, who was also at the presentation. "He has one of the sharpest minds I've seen in the industry in terms of focus and clarity."

To grow into a company that could compete internationally, Nelvana had to capture the attention of the major U.S. television networks. By getting Lucas's stamp of approval on the company, Nelvana did just that. "Lucas helped us establish ourselves in the U.S.," says Hirsh. "That was an important association because it eventually got us onto the networks."

The late 1970s were a transition period for Nelvana. Hirsh, Loubert, Smith, and company were now good enough to work for one of the most famous movie directors in the world, but they no longer qualified for a Visa card. As a result, Hirsh, then and still the company's chief travelling sales-man, was forced to live in high style while on the road. "We couldn't get Visas and regular credit cards because we had a bad history with them," he explains. "The only card we could get was the Enroute card. When I went to

New York on my early business trips, the only hotel the card was good at was the Waldorf Astoria, which is one of the most expensive hotels. Because I didn't have a regular credit card, we had to spend more money than we wanted to."

While Hirsh was living in luxury on the road, he and the other Nelvana employees were working in squalor at home. By the end of the 1970s, Nelvana had outgrown the little studio on King Street and moved into a decrepit old warehouse on Queens Quay, overlooking the Toronto water-front. Gerry Wills, the candle maker, had discovered that spacious and very cheap accommodation was available there and had alerted Loubert, his Toronto Island neighbour. The other tenants were wholesalers of such items as Oriental carpets, cheese, olives, and coffee. Non-paying tenants included a large rodent population and what some Nelvana staffers referred to as a "psycho" cat.

Mary Bertoia went to work for Nelvana in 1976. She recalls her first visit to the Queens Quay building. "I started walking through this maze of corridors, looking for Nelvana. It was dark, and there was this putrid olive smell everywhere. I thought, This is nuts, I can't work here. Then I found Nelvana. It was like an illusion, this rush of people working, and the atmosphere was warm and colourful. It was just so neat." She still works at Nelvana as a producer of still art for advertisements.

Veteran staffers like Bertoia and director Larry Jacobs remember the Queens Quay days as a time when Nelvana seemed like one big family. At the time, the company was concentrating on its holiday shows, dubbed the "Hallmark specials," and employees would work long hours for four months at a time and then be laid off. "A lot of us did a lot of different things at the beginning," says Jacobs. "I worked at my wife's pottery."

There were only about 50 employees; all of them were young, and few had started families. They had the stamina to work long hours and still have time left over to hang out together. Long evenings were spent at The Skipper, a restaurant in the same building. The entire staff could congregate around a few tables. They consumed large amounts of alcohol; other stimulants were often for sale in the washroom. Rob Kirkpatrick, now Nelvana's director of post-production, recalls liberating large quantities of toothpicks from The Skipper because they were useful for painting things too small to be painted by even the smallest brush.

The Queens Quay warehouse could never be faulted for being a sterile work environment; on the contrary, it overflowed with atmosphere, sometimes too much for the staff's liking. "If you walked in there after a night of drinking, the first thing that hit you was the smell of rotten fish," recalls Jacobs. "The fish were on the first floor, and we were on the second floor next to the Greek food importer. So you would pass the fish, then you would get into the olives and cheese."

The dank passageways connecting the different enterprises in the warehouse were equipped with rat traps, so Nelvana parlance for "Let's go for a smoke" became "Let's go check the traps." The traps, of course, were there for a good reason. Clive Smith recalls that they stopped setting mouse traps in the studio during production of the Halloween special *The Devil and Daniel Mouse* because it disturbed some of the animators to be drawing mice and killing them at the same time.

The waterfront was isolated from the rest of the city. During the winter, it got the worst of the weather because of the blistering winds that roared in off the lake. Mary Bertoia remembers a night when the combination of work to be finished and a

(LEFT) VETERAN ANIMATOR SCOTT GLYNN USES HIS OWN FACIAL EXPRESSION AS A REFERENCE FOR ANIMATION. (BELOW) FRANK NISSEN AND CLIVE SMITH CONTINUED DESIGN DISCUSSIONS OVER DINNER AT THE SKIPPER.

The Skipper
SEAFOOD RESTAURANT & TAVERN

GERRY WILLS STILL SERVES THE FAMOUS FRIDAY SPECIAL—CHILI (2001).

Friday Special
CHILLI
COMES WITH CHIPS
AND BREAD. $4.75
SMALL—$4.75
LARGE—$5.25

SOUP: CREAMY
TOMATO. SM-2.00
LG-2.50

the building wanted to renovate it and turn it into an upscale complex of expensive shops, offices, and apartments to be called the Terminal Warehouse. "We had a lease that ran another year," recalls Loubert. "But they wanted us out. To make life difficult, they started to do construction right next to the animators. Somebody was running a jackhammer. We had *The Star* come down and take pictures of the animators wearing hard hats and ear protectors. That hit the papers the next day. They said, 'OK, what do you want to get out of the lease?' I asked for our moving costs. In retrospect, we let them out of the lease for next to nothing."

It was time for Nelvana to move on, and not just to a new building. The company had done six successful half-hour TV specials and it had run out of holidays to do specials about. Its name was starting to become known in the industry, and its work had been seen around the world. Now it was time to do something more challenging and interesting than a half-hour TV show. It was time to make a feature film.

fierce storm outside persuaded some staffers to stay overnight. "We were painting all night and making dozens of pots of coffee. Meanwhile, windows were popping out of the building." Because of the isolated location, Nelvana had to provide its employees with a cafeteria. Loubert hired Wills to run it because he had been trained as a cook in prison, where he had served time for a misdemeanour. "I had no experience whatsoever," admits Wills. "Our budget allowed us to buy a used folding table, and I bought some pots at a Goodwill store." Wills's skills as a chef developed over the years; his chili, which he still serves every Friday at Nelvana, is legendary.

Nelvana's Queens Quay period ended with the 1970s. The owners of

WHEN IT WAS A NELVANA PROJECT, WE KNEW WE DIDN'T HAVE TO WORRY. IT WOULD BE THE BEST, THE VERY BEST. THANKS FOR MAKING US LOOK SO GOOD THESE MANY YEARS.

SHEILA NEVINS, EXECUTIVE VICE-PRESIDENT, ORIGINAL PROGRAMMING, HBO

WHEN WE DECIDED TO TAKE STAR WARS AND DEAL WITH IT IN AN ANIMATED FASHION FOR SATURDAY MORNING TELEVISION, I REALLY WANTED TO GET THE HIGHEST QUALITY ANIMATION COMPANY. I WANTED THEM TO TAKE OVER THE PROJECT AND GIVE US A GOOD PRODUCT WITHOUT LUCASFILM HAVING TO DO A LOT OF DRAMA CONTROL AND SUPERVISION. AND AFTER SURVEYING ALL OF THE ANIMATION COMPANIES THAT EXISTED AT THAT POINT IN TIME, I FELT THAT NELVANA HAD THE MOST TALENTED DIRECTORS AND ANIMATORS WORKING IN SATURDAY MORNING TELEVISION.

I'VE KIND OF WATCHED THEM FROM AFAR AS THEY HAVE GROWN UP. I VISITED THEM IN CANADA A FEW TIMES AND I KNEW ALL THE PEOPLE THERE IN THE BEGINNING, BUT JUST AS MY COMPANY HAS GROWN UP TO BE THIS GIANT COMPANY, THEY HAVE ALSO HAD THAT SAME TRAJECTORY. IT IS ALWAYS INTERESTING TO WATCH COMPANIES THAT YOU HAVE FAITH IN GROW AND PROSPER AND FULFILL THEIR POTENTIAL.

GEORGE LUCAS, LUCASFILM

THE CRITICAL WORDS, CREATIVE COLLABORATION AND GENEROUS COOPERATION, PERHAPS BEST SUM UP THE PLEASURE OF WORKING WITH NELVANA; CRITICAL WORDS INDEED WHEN ONE SETS OUT TO CREATE SO VAST A PROJECT AS PUTTING TOGETHER AN ANIMATED FEATURE FROM SCRATCH. THUS PROVIDING TIME TO LEARN, MAKE MISTAKES, AND MAKE NEW FRIENDS.

MAURICE SENDAK

NELVANA IS A CROWN JEWEL. IT'S AN EXAMPLE OF CREATIVITY, ENTREPRENEURSHIP AND GOVERNMENT POLICY IN PERFECT HARMONY. THE ABSENCE OF ANY ONE OF THESE THREE ELEMENTS AND THE HISTORY OF NELVANA IS NOT A BOOK, IT'S A VERY SHORT STORY.

JOHN CASSADAY, PRESIDENT AND CHIEF EXECUTIVE OFFICER, CORUS ENTERTAINMENT INC.

CHAPTER 2 THE 1980s

One of many Web sites devoted to *Rock & Rule* proclaims it "the best animated film of all time." Not even Clive Smith, who spent the first three years of the 1980s immersed in the job of directing Nelvana's first feature film would make so extravagant a claim. Most of the people who worked on *Rock & Rule* consider it a flawed but fascinating movie that contains flashes of brilliance. That it still retains an impassioned cult following, almost 20 years after its release, is proof of its enduring qualities.

Both from an artistic and a financial point of view, *Rock & Rule* was serious moviemaking, light years away from the trifles such as *Zounds of Music* that Nelvana had made when it was just starting out. *Rock & Rule* was a full-length musical, with state-of-the-art animation and famous musicians, aimed at an older, more sophisticated, and more demanding audience than anything Nelvana had previously produced.

By going ahead with *Rock & Rule*, Nelvana was behaving like a gambler who has enjoyed a few modest victories and then risks everything on a single roll of the dice. If he wins, he's rich; if he loses, he's broke.

It was a huge risk but one worth taking. Smith explains: "We had grown the company with a lot of talent from Sheridan [College] and we were at the point where we needed to do something bigger, something more exciting, and use some of the skills that were developed making those television specials."

The concept for a post-apocalyptic rock and roll musical was Patrick Loubert's. His original name for it was *D-rats*. The D-rats were a race of mutants formed when rats combined with humans in the aftermath of a nuclear war. The story revolves around a beautiful D-rat named Angel and an evil one named Mok, a legendary rock star and Mick Jagger lookalike. Mok is trying to decipher an ancient code to unlock a doorway to another world. He has almost succeeded but needs one last thing—a special voice. Then he hears a singing performance by Angel, voiced in the film by Deborah Harry, lead singer of Blondie, a popular rock group of the 1970s. He realizes she has the voice he has been searching for, kidnaps her, and takes her to Nuke York.

The atmosphere of the movie is dark, desperate, and cynical—more like *Blade Runner* than *Cosmic Christmas*. And yet it didn't start out that way. "When we originally developed *D-rats*, it was a kids' film for a much younger audience," recalls Smith. "It was a softer kind of story, a

(RIGHT) LOUBERT, SMITH, AND DENNIS BROWN SET UP A SHOT FOR ROCK & RULE. (BELOW) FRANK NISSEN EXPLORED A VARIETY OF IDEAS FOR THE DESIGN OF THE D-RATS. SHOWN HERE ARE EARLY IDEAS FOR ANGEL, FROM ROCK & RULE.

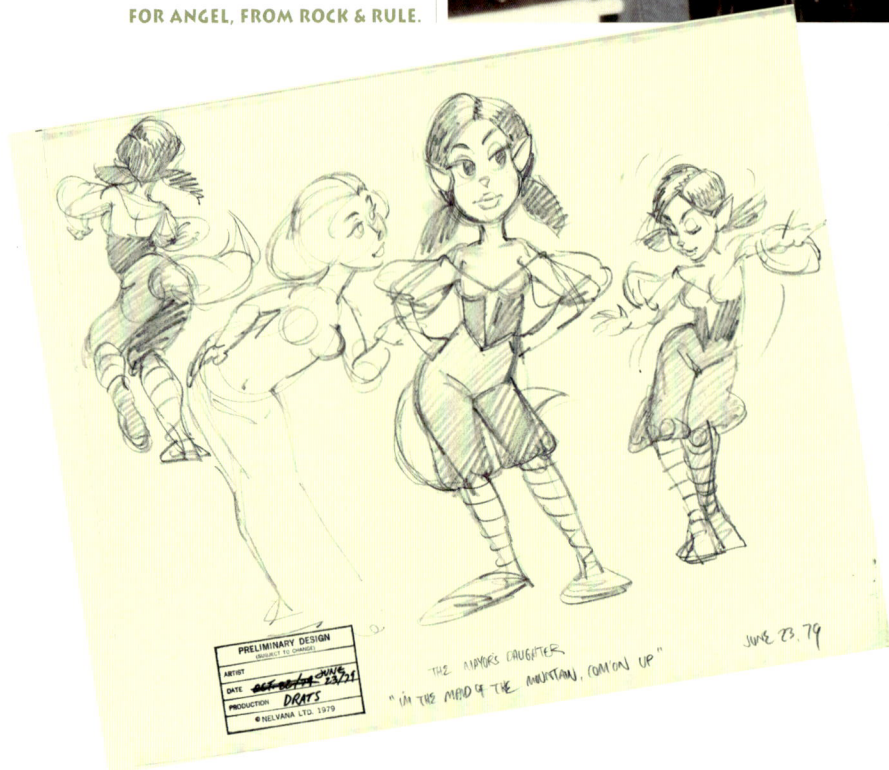

PRELIMINARY DESIGN
(SUBJECT TO CHANGE)
ARTIST
DATE
PRODUCTION DRATS
© NELVANA LTD. 1979

THE MAYORS DAUGHTER
"IN THE MIND OF THE MOUNTAIN, COM'ON UP"

JUNE 23, 79

They listened to the writers and spent almost four years making an edgy, animated rock musical for sophisticated teens. From an artistic standpoint, this was more interesting than another project for the under-10 crowd. But from a business stand-point, did it make sense? Loubert points out that in Europe everybody watches animated movies. "They always have," he says. "Adults, kids, any age group. But here, adults wouldn't watch animation."

They wouldn't, that is, unless they were taking their kids to see it. But *Rock & Rule* wasn't *Bambi*. It was aimed at rebellious teens who didn't need their parents to take them to the movies and who weren't in the habit of going to animated movies on their own. Making a feature was in itself risky for a small studio. Magnifying the risk was the fact that Nelvana was trying to create a new market for animation among people who thought they had outgrown it.

But there were positive signs as well. Comic books for adults, long popular in Europe and Japan, were starting to make inroads in North America. The *Heavy Metal* comics were aimed at young adults, and Canadian producer Ivan Reitman was making an animated movie based on them. (Reitman wanted Nelvana to get

medieval world rather than the high-tech, gritty, steel-and-concrete world we ended up with. The D-rats were different, a little more cartoony."

Before committing to this concept, Nelvana consulted with outside experts. "Patrick and I spent time with George Lucas and picked his brain about what he thought would work in an anima-tion feature," recalls Hirsh. "He thought animated comedies were where an independent could succeed. Unfortun-ately, we didn't listen to him enough. We did a music picture instead."

Two Canadian screenwriters from Hollywood arrived in Toronto to give their advice. "They said we were going for the wrong market," recalls Smith. "They said the movie should be for teenagers. And that it should be much more edgy."

involved in *Heavy Metal,* but the studio, already well into pre-production on *D-rats,* turned him down.)

The biggest hits in movies or any other art form, says Smith, are usually the most original, the ones that don't rely on market research, those that "come out of left field." He and his collaborators thought *Rock & Rule* would be one of those. "We were totally naive—we thought people were going to love it because it was brand new, because it was fresh. That's not the way a marketing person thinks. A marketing person thinks, What do people want to see? What are the demographics?"

If anyone at Nelvana had asked the latter question, it might have curbed their enthusiasm. By 1983, the youth culture that had been such a powerful force during the 1960s and 1970s was dying, not because the artists contributing to it had run out of steam but because the baby boomers had grown up. By the time *Rock & Rule* was released, the boomers were aged 17 to 36. Most of them were too old to appreciate a movie like *Rock & Rule.* The teenagers of 1983 were those born during the "baby bust" that followed the boom. The bust is a much smaller population cohort than the boom, so *Rock & Rule* was targeted at a shrinking market.

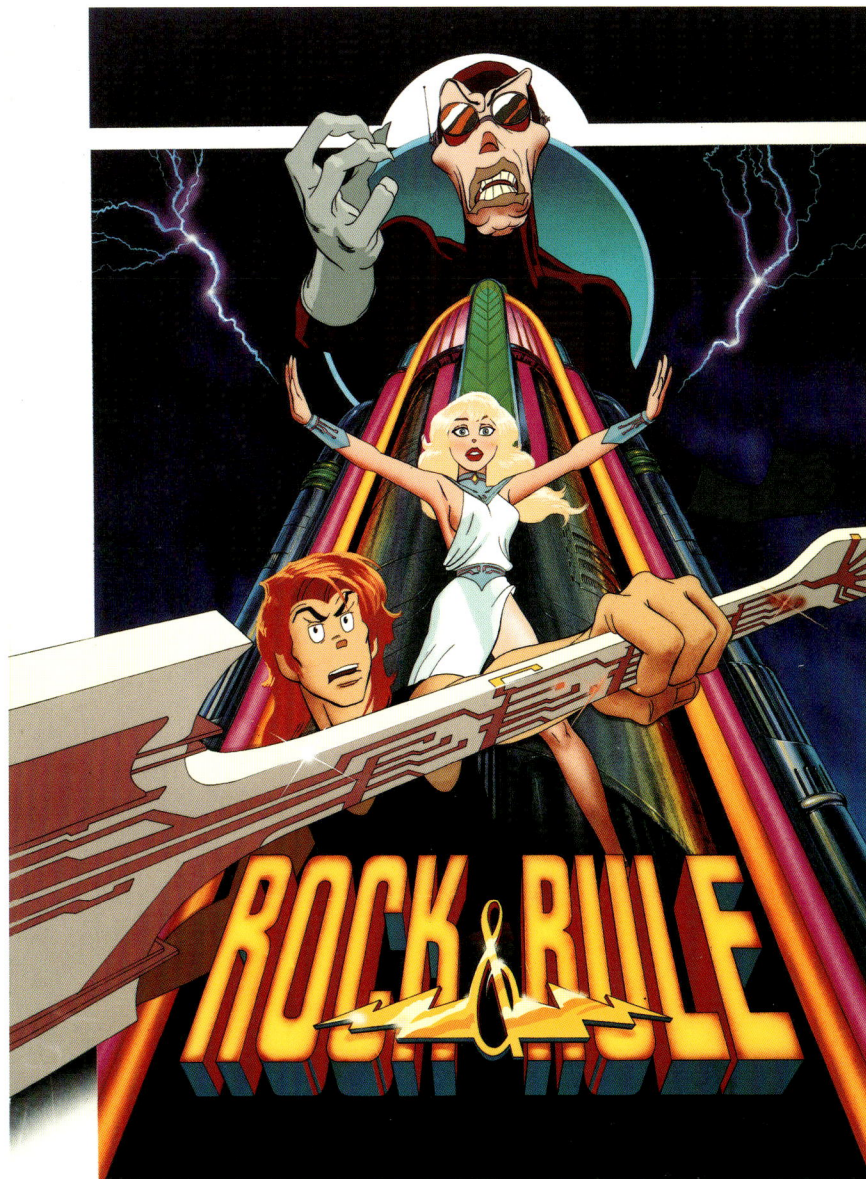

Still, investors thought well enough of the project to invest $5 million in it. To raise that kind of money, Nelvana needed outside help. *Rock & Rule* marked the beginning of Michael Harrison's long relationship with Nelvana. Harrison, an investment dealer who would become chairman of the board when Nelvana later became a public company, travelled across Canada with a 16 mm projector to show prospective investors highlights of the holiday specials. In addition to extolling the virtues of

Nelvana's moviemaking, he explained how investing in *Rock & Rule* could reduce a person's tax bill. To encourage a Canadian film industry, the federal government had introduced a system of credits whereby investors could reduce their taxes by the amount of their investment in a film project. In return for their money, they received units of a limited partnership set up to make the film. Even with the tax credits, it wasn't easy to scare up $5 million; without them, it would have been impossible.

Thanks to Harrison, Nelvana's filmmakers got the money they needed. Now all they had to do was make the movie. At the beginning, they had no idea how huge a task they had set themselves. "We were trying to move from television animation to feature film animation," recalls Loubert. "A feature is more sophisticated—more movement, more drawings, more people on the screen, more special effects. We did a lot of stuff that at the time was cutting-edge special effects. So we had raised the bar as far as animation

A BIG ANNUAL EVENT IS THE SUMMER PICNIC.
THIS PHOTO WAS TAKEN SUMMER 1989.

went, and we found that we couldn't do it to the sort of schedules and budgets that we had when we were doing half-hour television specials."

It was an expensive learning process. "*Rock & Rule* taught us that you had to start off with a locked script," Smith says. It wasn't that good movies hadn't been made before without a final script, *Casablanca* being the most famous case in point. But *Casablanca* had been a play before it was a movie, so at least its creators knew where they were going. On *Rock & Rule*, although there was a storyboard, the direction kept shifting. "An animator would be in the middle

of working on a scene and someone would come and take it off the light table and say, 'That's out now,'" recalls Peter Sauder, then as now a Nelvana screenwriter. "Michael [Hirsh] kept taking scenes to L.A. and getting them critiqued by the distributor. Then he would come back and there would be more changes."

Loubert says they decided to shoot without a script because Disney had done it successfully. He had brought Frank Thomas and Ollie Johnston, veteran Disney animators, to Toronto to help upgrade the skills of Nelvana's people. They advised Nelvana to "develop the characters

and run the characters through the plot and get a story. When we started to use that method, certain things would change. Certain things wouldn't work, and we would change the scene or rewrite. We were exploring the dynamics of an animated feature. We were trying to do it the same way that Disney did his pictures—but he had budgets from here to Pluto, and we didn't."

The gloomy and forbidding atmosphere of the world of the D-rats was attained with the use of some advanced special effects. The final result was impressive, but the process was arduous. "We didn't really know

what we were doing in special effects," Loubert recalls. "We had very sophisticated equipment but we didn't know how long it was going to take." One year became two, and two became three, and still the movie wasn't finished. Meanwhile, Reitman's *Heavy Metal*, which began production around the same time, was released in 1981.

The making of *Rock & Rule* was a chaotic, hectic process; the film-makers constantly felt they were running out of time and money. And yet the experience is remembered fondly by most of those involved, including the musicians. "It was freeing in a way because I didn't have to be me," says Iggy Pop in a documentary made later about the making of the film. Iggy Pop did the voice of the beast that Mok summons from another world at the end of the film. For Deborah Harry, it was also an exciting experience. Like many performers new to animation, she at first thought the character whose voice she was singing was a cartoon. But an animated character is not a cartoon, it's a person. "Michael Hirsh told us not to try to do things as if they were for a cartoon character," she says, "just to try and do them as if they were for yourself." Maurice White, of Earth Wind and Fire, wrote and performed one of the

(OPPOSITE PAGE) FROM ROCK & RULE. (LEFT) COMIC BOOK PUBLISHERS MARVEL PRODUCED A GRAPHIC NOVEL USING STILLS FROM THE FILM TO COINCIDE WITH THE 1983 RELEASE OF ROCK & RULE. BOOK ADAPTATION: BOB BUDIANSKY AND CLIVE SMITH. BOOK DESIGN: CLIVE SMITH WITH LAURA SHEPARD AND KATE SHEPARD. (BELOW) SKETCH FROM ROCK & RULE.

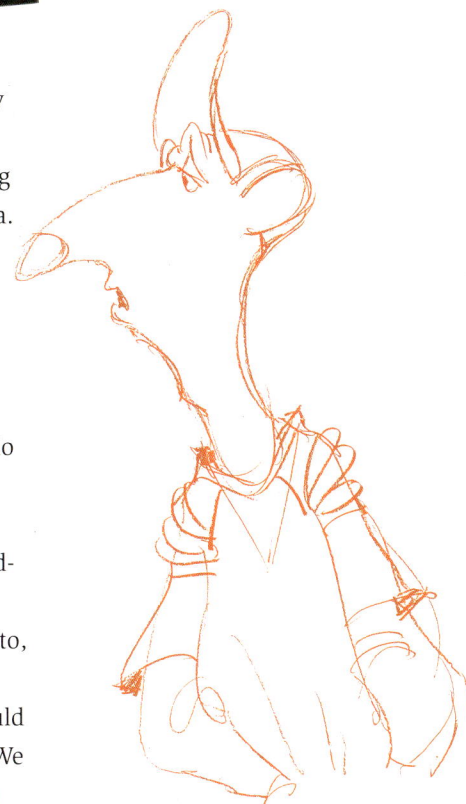

film's best musical scenes, set in a dance club called Club 666. "Some of the things that you can't do for real, you can do in animation," he says. "It takes our imaginations farther out, which I think is very beautiful."

Not that the musicians were always easy to work with. "I was involved in all the music sessions right through except those with Lou Reed [the musical voice of the villain Mok]," recalls Smith. "When I said I wanted to be there when he laid down the final vocals and did the final mix, he said, 'No, I don't allow anybody in the studio when I'm doing my final vocals. You're welcome to come down if you'd like to be sent back to Toronto in a number of boxes.' That

was said in true Mok fashion, totally in character."

Smith spent a lot of time chasing the musicians around North America. "The climax of the story is when Angel [Deborah Harry] and Omar, Angel's true love [voiced by Cheap Trick], sing together and beat the demon. But we couldn't get them [Harry and Cheap Trick] in the studio at the same time because both of them were really busy. Cheap Trick was playing 280 days a year. I recorded Cheap Trick in Chicago, their hometown, in Los Angeles, in Toronto, and in New York—I went wherever they were to pick up tracks. We would lay down a track and then decide, 'We need another verse,' and they would modify it. That's how we would build

the songs—you do it rough and see how it works and you modify it.

"For this big finale, Deborah and Chris Stein [Blondie's bass player] laid down the first bed track of the song. It starts off with Angel singing. I took these tracks from the Deborah Harry session in New York to the Cheap Trick session in Chicago for the engineer to tie in with another 24-track tape. It was a nightmare, but we did achieve it. We ended up with these two tracks, with Chris Stein's bass playing on one, kind of drifting, and the bass player from Cheap Trick on another, really driving. Added to that mix was the music by Patricia Cullen, who wrote the score for *Rock & Rule*. So we had three completely different musical entities building one finale song, in various different places. They were never in the same room at the same time."

Meanwhile, the animators back in Toronto were also getting plenty of attention. Nelvana organized acting classes for them. Animators were cast to "play" certain animated characters just as actors are cast to play "live" characters. So Angel was animated by a young woman, Anne-Marie Bardwell, who worked hard to prepare for her role: "I studied a lot of vocalists and used them as reference in performing—how they handled their instru-

ments, what moves they made, their facial expressions when they were singing. And then it was just up to me to take those and apply them, working with the personality of the character."

Nelvana needed another $1 million to finish the movie. This was a harder sell for Michael Harrison than raising the original money because this time there was no tax credit to mitigate the risk. "I had to lean on some friends and people I knew," he recalls. Harrison did manage to round up the money by issuing what today would be called junk bonds. Because the risk was so high, Nelvana had to pay a very high rate of interest and, in addition, surrender 25 per cent of the company to the lenders. "At that point, with the company worth just about nothing, this was an act of faith," Harrison recalls.

Finally, all the work was over and *Rock & Rule* was ready to be released. Optimism reigned. "We were so excited about it," recalls Smith. "I loved that film." And yet there were ominous signs. While Nelvana had been spending three and a half years making its movie, the MGM-United Artists executives who had agreed to distribute it had been replaced. Their replacements were not interested in *Rock & Rule*. "They gave us no support whatsoever," recalls Smith.

The ways of the movie industry are sometimes incomprehensible, even to those who work in it. Why would a distributor, who has everything to gain if a movie does well, not help to sell it to the public? Yet sometimes distributors give up on a movie even before it is released. Loubert had watched in dismay in 1969 as this happened to his hero, Gillo Pontecorvo, whose political thriller *Burn!*, starring Marlon Brando as an English adventurer who instigates a slave rebellion on a Caribbean island, was dumped with no publicity into action movie houses and disappeared before its intended audience even knew it existed.

Smith and animator Frank Nissen went to Boston, one of three U.S. cities where *Rock & Rule* would be test-marketed by the distributors, to try to drum up publicity, since the distributor was providing none. Smith rented a car, which he plastered with *Rock & Rule* posters. The pair drove around town and did radio and television interviews. They visited the various Boston university campuses, where they did two-hour presentations on how the movie was made. They did everything they could think of to try to reach the people most likely to appreciate their movie.

Michael Harrison, whose investors had $6 million on the line, still has vivid memories of opening night. He was among a dozen people involved in *Rock & Rule* who went to Boston for the occasion. "It was in six theatres, so we split up to cover all the theatres. I went to one theatre with one other person from Nelvana. Other than us, there were six people in the theatre. Afterward, we added up the total attendance in the six theatres and it was fewer than 50. We knew then we weren't going to have a huge success."

The theatre Clive Smith went to had only four non-Nelvana people in the audience. "That's a killer when you've spent three and a half years," he says. "I was devastated, totally devastated." Making matters worse was a review that called the animation "very limited." For Smith, that was rubbing salt in an open wound. "It made me so mad. We could be faulted on many things but not the animation quality." He retreated to Nantucket Island, an isolated outpost off Cape Cod. "I just hid for two weeks. I couldn't face anything. I didn't know why it hadn't worked."

Two decades later, he does know why *Rock & Rule* didn't work. "*D-rats* became *Rock & Rule* as we started to take the advice of those famous writers—I can't even remember who they were. And we changed the picture and we got it darker and darker and darker. It was so bloody dark it just fell between the cracks. There was no market. Animation today is more popular, it appeals to a wide audience, it has a completely different identity. In those days, animation was for kids—it was as simple as that. When kids turn 12 or 13, they are turning their backs on their childhood. They were not going to go see an animated movie. Why didn't we get that? I have no idea. We were stupid."

GROUPIE IN NUKE YORK, *ROCK & RULE*.

Hirsh agrees that older kids are more difficult to reach than the younger kids who had enjoyed *Cosmic Christmas* and *The Devil and Daniel Mouse* on television. "We made a fundamental error in terms of where we went," he says. And yet the partners' decision to raise their sights wasn't necessarily misguided. "We had been making specials and we thought it was the natural evolution to produce a feature, that it would give us more prestige as a studio, give us a bigger platform, be a company-building opportunity. If it had worked, that's what it would have been. The problem with features is that if you fail, it's much worse than failing in TV because the stakes are higher."

Rock & Rule did get shown on CBC television. And it lives on as a cult classic. "I get calls all the time from people wanting interviews about *Rock & Rule*," says Loubert. Smith also gets calls and e-mails from fans wanting to see the movie re-released into theatres. In a sense, there is a parallel here with *Pinocchio, Dumbo,* and *Fantasia* in that those animation classics also started life as box office failures. However, unlike *Rock & Rule*, the Disney movies eventually did make money. *Rock & Rule* is still a money loser but, nevertheless, it was an important step toward Nelvana's eventual success. With *Rock & Rule*, Nelvana became serious about the art of moviemaking. And when *Rock & Rule* failed financially, the company was finally forced to get serious about the business of moviemaking.

Albert Einstein once said, "In the middle of difficulty lies opportunity." One did not need Einstein's brain to realize that Nelvana, in the aftermath of *Rock & Rule*, was in the middle of difficulty. "It left us technically bankrupt," says Hirsh. "We didn't go bankrupt, but by any accountant's view we were." Hirsh calls the post– *Rock & Rule* period, 1983 to 1986, Nelvana's "dark years." Adds Loubert: "We went to the wall for that film, bet the studio on it, and everything else that we had at that time." And what did they have to show for their big gamble? A million dollars of debt and the loss of 25 per cent of the company they had been building for more than a decade. And the loss as well of a building they had owned on Lake Shore Boulevard, beneath the Gardiner Expressway, where they had moved their studios from Queens Quay.

The only profitable part of the company at the time was a division called Nelvana Animated Commercials (NAC), run by Bob Fortier, who had originally joined the company as an animator on *The Devil and Daniel Mouse*. As if things weren't bad enough, Fortier, in the wake of the *Rock & Rule* debacle, left Nelvana, taking the commercial business with him.

The company was fortunate that the CIBC did not force it into bankruptcy. "The bank will only let you go so far," says Loubert. "This was a business, the film business, that wasn't really a business then. I think we came very close to going bankrupt." The main reason the bank didn't pull the plug was that Michael Harrison and the holders of the debt that had been issued to allow *Rock & Rule* to finish asked it not to.

So times were tough, but it wasn't as if the partners weren't used to adversity. Nelvana had never been a big moneymaker. As Loubert recalls, to that point in the company's life, his major preoccupation had not been making a profit but rather making the weekly payroll. "I still have nightmares about making the payroll," he says. "I remember having to go to people and say, 'Listen, the good news is you're getting a cheque, but the bad news is you can't cash it for 10 days.' We used to have group meetings where I would say, 'OK, you can cash your cheques, not tomorrow but the day after.' People were generally pretty good about it. And we did pay everybody."

After the *Rock & Rule* fiasco, the partners decided they had to be upfront with their major creditors. "We were in a situation," says Hirsh, "where either we could go bankrupt or we could stick with it and see if we could pay down the debt. We decided

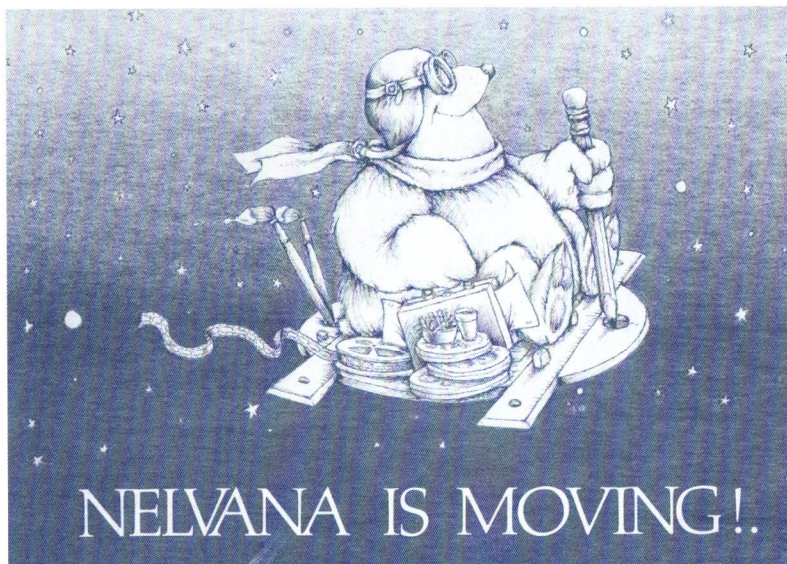

NELVANA IS MOVING!

that if the suppliers would go with us, we would work ourselves out of the debt. We went to see all of our key suppliers, said we were in financial trouble, and that we would try to work ourselves out. They said they would stick with us."

The exception was Quinn Labs, a film laboratory that was in financial trouble itself. Loubert persuaded another lab, Film House, to buy Nelvana's debt from Quinn, and Nelvana moved its business there.

Getting some time from the creditors was the first part of the survival strategy. The second part was finding ways to make money fast so that Nelvana could pay its debts and establish itself on sound financial footing.

MARCH 11 1980

FINAL DESIGN

ARTIST SCOTT.

DATE *June 20/80*

PRODUCTION

That meant finding a lot of work, which in turn meant Nelvana could not be too picky about which projects it chose to take on.

The holiday specials and *Rock & Rule* were "proprietary" productions, meaning that Nelvana owned them and could re-release them at any time. They were Nelvana's own original concepts, and all the creative work on them had been done in-house. In the long run, doing one's own shows is a more profitable strategy, as well as being a more satisfying creative experience. But "service work" on other companies' productions brings in money faster.

So Hirsh went out and started hustling business. It was a classic example of the saying that knowing one is going to be hanged the next morning concentrates the mind wonderfully. Until that time, Nelvana had never produced more than one hour of television programming in one year. In 1983, it sold 100 hours. Almost overnight, out of necessity, Nelvana transformed itself from a craft producer to a mass producer.

Jamie Kellner, who had syndicated *Cosmic Christmas*, had moved to Orion Pictures (since absorbed by Metro-Goldwyn-Mayer), which was making a live action TV show called *Twenty Minute Workout*, an exercise program featuring gorgeous young women. Kellner gave Nelvana the contract to make 65 half-hours of *Twenty Minute Workout*. It became a much talked about hit and developed a big following, particularly among males who had never before shown an interest in fitness.

The other major contract was for an animated kids' series called *Inspector Gadget*®, being produced by DiC Entertainment, a Franco-American company operating out of Los Angeles and Paris. It was about a bumbling police inspector whose incompetence is offset by a niece and a dog, who do the real investigative work. As part of the deal, Nelvana obtained Canadian rights to the show, which Hirsh sold to First Choice, predecessor of The Movie Network. "That deal really helped save Nelvana," he says. "There was a lot of work and a lot of profit for us."

Like *Rock & Rule*, Nelvana's first feature, *Inspector Gadget*, its first series, was a challenge for the creative staff. Because they were learning as they went along, the process of making *Inspector Gadget* was as chaotic as the making of *Rock & Rule*. Not only was this Nelvana's first series, it was also the first time it had collaborated with another company and its first show in which the animation was done overseas. Storyboards were written in Toronto and the voices recorded. The storyboards and recordings were then shipped to Japan, where the manual animation took place under the supervision of Dave and Dale Cox, two senior Nelvana employees. This, in turn, came back to Toronto to be assembled into the finished product.

Suddenly, instead of a large number of animators working on one story (250 people had laboured on *Rock & Rule*), Nelvana needed a large number of writers working on many different stories. "It was insane," recalls writer Peter Sauder. "If Patrick saw some graffiti on the washroom and found out who wrote it, suddenly that person was a writer. *Inspector Gadget* was what brought all the employees back (who had been laid off after *Rock & Rule*). But the shocker for animators was that they had to learn how to storyboard because there was no animation going on. Everybody wrote, including the ink and paint guys."

Sauder, one of the first graduates of the Sheridan College program, had begun his career as an animator, coming to work at Nelvana during the 1970s. Late one night, while drawing a scene of the holiday special *Easter Fever*, he had what he describes as "an epiphany"—he realized he couldn't draw. It was a shocking revelation because none of his teachers at Sheridan had ever mentioned it.

As Patrick Loubert passed his table, Sauder said, "I can't draw."

Loubert said, "Yes, you can."

Sauder says now: "Patrick knew I couldn't draw. What he meant was that he needed a body making no money sitting in a chair doing some footage."

The *Inspector Gadget* assignment coincided with the dawn of the personal computer age, so a computer was acquired to speed up production. "It had a green screen," Sauder recalls. "Nobody knew how to use it. So it sat there while we were typing away on old Selectric typewriters and cutting and pasting. Nobody knew anything about scriptwriting. We winged it."

Inspector Gadget taught Nelvana how to get product out the door quickly. In animation, the script has to be the same length as the finished product. The director of an animated program does not have the luxury enjoyed by a live action director, who can shoot as much as he wants and cut the film down to size later. In an animated show, the voices are recorded first and then the drawings are matched to the recordings. This means that most of the editing takes place before the movie is shot, rather than afterward. When DiC sent in a 45-page script, Nelvana's novice storyboarders had to reshape it to an appropriate length. "There was no time to go back to the writer," Sauder says, "so we had to rewrite."

A key player in this process was the creator of the Gadget character, Jean Chalopin, one of the partners in DiC, who was constantly on the go, from Los Angeles to Tokyo to Paris to Toronto. Chalopin would send 30-foot-long telexes telling Nelvana's novice writers how to rewrite a story. Most of the stories were supplied by outside writers, but the finished product rarely resembled anything they wrote. "When it was all finished," says Sauder, "and we had actually pulled it off, we said, 'Let's do it again knowing what we are doing.'"

That's exactly what the owners of Nelvana intended to do. Michael Hirsh puts it in perspective: "From 1970 to 1977, almost nothing happened here. From

1977 to 1982, we made our first shows that travelled around the world and started to build a name for Nelvana. Then, starting in 1983, you started to see a real industrial beehive of activity. The company had made a decision to be serious."

In its new businesslike approach, Nelvana began looking for ways to exploit the synergies that exist between animated TV and movie characters and other products. It began forging links to the toy industry. Nelvana made four TV shows about a doll named Strawberry Shortcake. This was not the kind of creative filmmaking that Hirsh, Loubert, and Smith had aspired to when they started Nelvana. In fact, as Loubert admits, these shows were little more than "vehicles for the advertiser."

But the shows helped pay off the debt and were useful in another important way as well—as part of a learning process in which Nelvana was groping its way toward a strategy that eventually would allow it to combine quality and profitability. The company's brain trust was beginning to understand that you cannot re-invent the wheel for each program. Instead, you can take an existing character, such as a doll or the hero of a book, and make a program for millions of kids already familiar with

that character. Doing that doesn't guarantee box office success—nothing can—but it does improve the odds.

Nelvana has shown over the years that it can be versatile. *Twenty Minute Workout*, targeted at an adult audience, was a hit, and in 1986 the company would produce a live action feature for adults, *The Burglar*, starring Whoopi Goldberg. It would also make several live action TV series for school-age kids, including *The Hardy Boys*, *Nancy Drew*, and *The Edison Twins*. But a company, like a person, can be versatile and still be especially good at one thing. The one thing Nelvana is especially good at is entertaining very young children. In 1985, a movie based on some stuffed toys called Care Bears drove that point home once and for all.

The Care Bears were creations of Those Characters from Cleveland, Inc., a unit of American Greetings Corp. Hirsh knew that a movie about the bears was being planned and he wanted it for Nelvana. Other companies also wanted the job, including Nelvana's *Inspector Gadget* partner, DiC, the front-runner because it had already done 13 TV episodes about the Care Bears. On the other hand, Nelvana had recent experience making a feature.

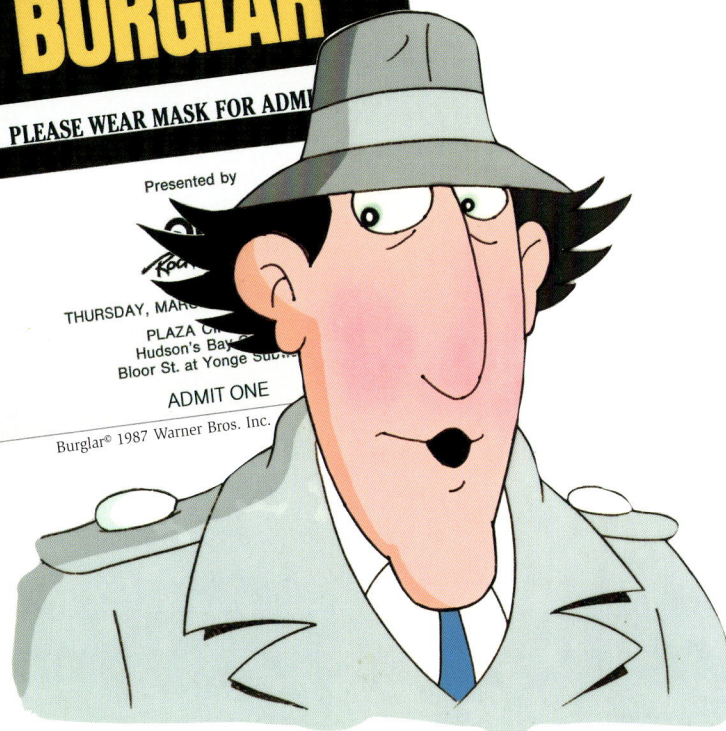

YOU ARE CORDIALLY INVITED
TO SNEAK IN
TO A SNEAK PREVIEW

WHOOPI GOLDBERG

BURGLAR

PLEASE WEAR MASK FOR ADMI

Presented by

THURSDAY, MAR

PLAZA C
Hudson's Bay
Bloor St. at Yonge

ADMIT ONE

Burglar© 1987 Warner Bros. Inc.

(OPPOSITE PAGE) BEETLEJUICE, BASED ON THE CHARACTER CREATED BY TIM BURTON, WAS THE STAR OF THE NELVANA SERIES OF THE SAME NAME. DESIGN: ROBIN BUDD AND JOHN HALFPENNY.
(LEFT) IN 1986, WHOOPI GOLDBERG AND BOBCAT GOLDTHWAIT STARRED IN BURGLAR, A LIVE ACTION FILM DEVELOPED BY NELVANA AND ON WHICH THEY SHARE A PRODUCER'S CREDIT. (BELOW) INSPECTOR GADGET WAS NELVANA'S INTRODUCTION TO THE WORLD OF TELEVISION SERIES AND OVERSEAS PRODUCTION.

THE EDISON TWNS LOGO. (BELOW) STRAWBERRY SHORTCAKE STARRED IN HER OWN SERIES OF FOUR HALF-HOUR SPECIALS.

And it had the services of a writer, Peter Sauder, whose work on *Strawberry Shortcake* was admired by the Care Bears people. As a result, Nelvana got a contract to produce a script for the Care Bears movie. Now all Hirsh had to do was persuade the producers, a partnership of Those Characters from Cleveland and Kenner Toys, to let Nelvana make the movie as well.

He had to come up with a pitch that would distinguish Nelvana from the other contenders. He decided to do one based on the Pepsi challenge advertising campaign that was on TV at the time, in which people were asked to participate in a blind tasting of cola drinks and choose the one they preferred. Hirsh took clips of all the contenders' work and broke them down into the different components, including animation quality, music, sound effects, and colour. He then

asked the producers to choose which was best. Nelvana scored higher than any of its opponents.

"Because they were all Madison Avenue people, they thought mine was the best pitch," says Hirsh. "They said, 'We know you've rigged this against everybody else because you've chosen the clips. But we like the approach.'" The clincher for Nelvana was that the president of a competing firm accidentally had his fly open during his presentation, which, Hirsh heard later, turned off some of the women at the meeting.

Mistakes are valuable because you learn from them, and Nelvana was determined not to repeat the mistakes of *Rock & Rule*. *Care Bears* would be brought in on time and on budget. So while *Rock & Rule* had taken three years and more than $6 million to make, *Care Bears* was completed in eight months during 1984 for half as much money. "Nobody had ever made an animated movie for theatrical release for as little money and in as little time," says Hirsh.

It wasn't done easily. The *Care Bears* movie was Nelvana's first experience with contracting out animation to Asia, and because of language and cultural differences, things didn't always go smoothly. By this time, most of the animation industry had

moved the labour-intensive part of its production offshore to take advantage of lower costs, and Nelvana found itself competing with other companies for the attention of the South Korean studios. Smith and Loubert had to spend extended periods in South Korea ensuring that the work got done. For Smith, this involved collaborating with Korean directors who could not speak English. He recalls a typical misunderstanding in which he used the expression "We'll just cheat it in," meaning that a problem could be solved quickly by making some minor alteration to one of the animation cels. When this was translated by Smith's interpreter, the director got upset. "In the translation, this word 'cheat' was very bad. We had a conversation [to try to clarify the misunderstanding] that must have gone on for 20 minutes. That sort of thing happened often."

Far more serious was the disappearance of the layouts without which the animation for *Care Bears* could not be done. A group of animators who had not been paid walked out and took the layouts with them. Loubert had no choice but to buy them back. David Altman, who is now Nelvana's 3-D technology director, was in South Korea with Loubert and Smith at the time. One of his jobs was to carry around a hockey bag containing US$20,000 in Korean yuan. "They would only do business in cash," Loubert says. "David, Clive, and I went around in the middle of the night and knocked on doors. People wouldn't open their door until I showed them the money. They'd give us the layouts back and I'd give them the yuan. This went on for three nights."

By this time, the movie was well behind schedule, a schedule that had to be met because a theatrical release date was already set. Loubert sent half the work to Taiwan under the supervision of Lenora Hume, director of production at the time and who now works for Disney. He and Smith stayed in Korea with the other half.

Getting the work done was hard but getting it out of the country was just as challenging. Using normal channels, moving merchandise through customs and security could take as long as two weeks. Fortunately, the studio, so unreliable when it came to getting the work done, had a dependable system for circumventing the red tape. A box filled with junk would be sent to the airport several days in advance. The box would be cleared for export, with all the right stamps on it and the correct forms filled out. It would stay at the airport until the

(LEFT) THE CARE BEARS ADVENTURE IN WONDERLAND.
(BELOW) DAVE COX SPENT MONTHS AS NELVANA'S EYES IN JAPAN, OVERSEEING PRODUCTION ON INSPECTOR GADGET.

film was ready to go. Then the film would be delivered to the airport, the box would be sliced open, the junk taken out and replaced with the film, and the box sent on its way. The hockey bag full of yuan helped facilitate this process.

But just because the film had escaped Korea didn't necessarily mean it was home-free. Loubert recalls an occasion in which he was accompanying footage that had not yet been exposed. He had to change planes in

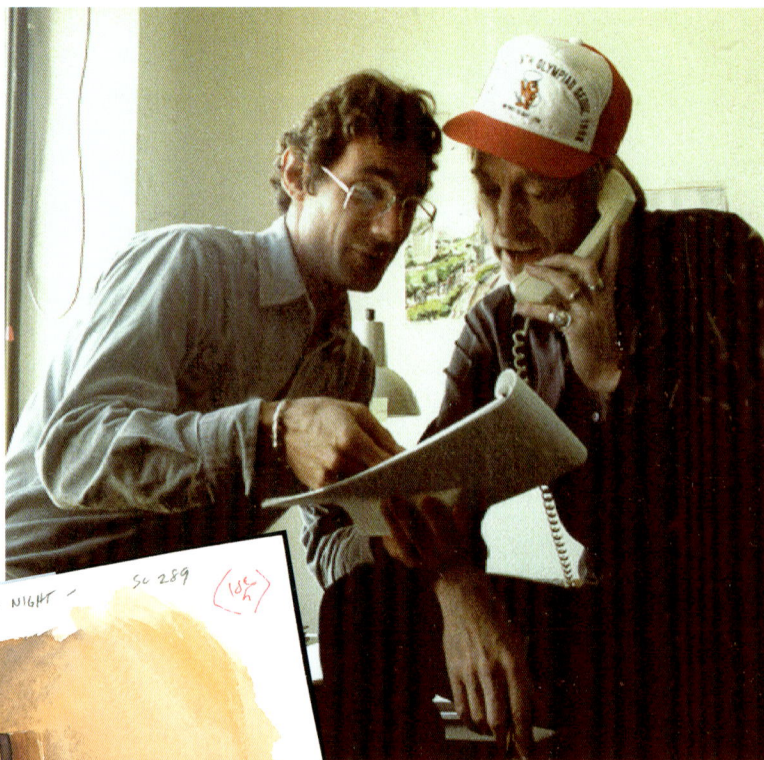

(RIGHT) SMITH AND DAVID ALTMAN IN KOREA, 1985. (BELOW) TYPICAL COLOUR SKETCH, WITH NOTES, USED IN DEVELOPING ANIMATED SEQUENCES.

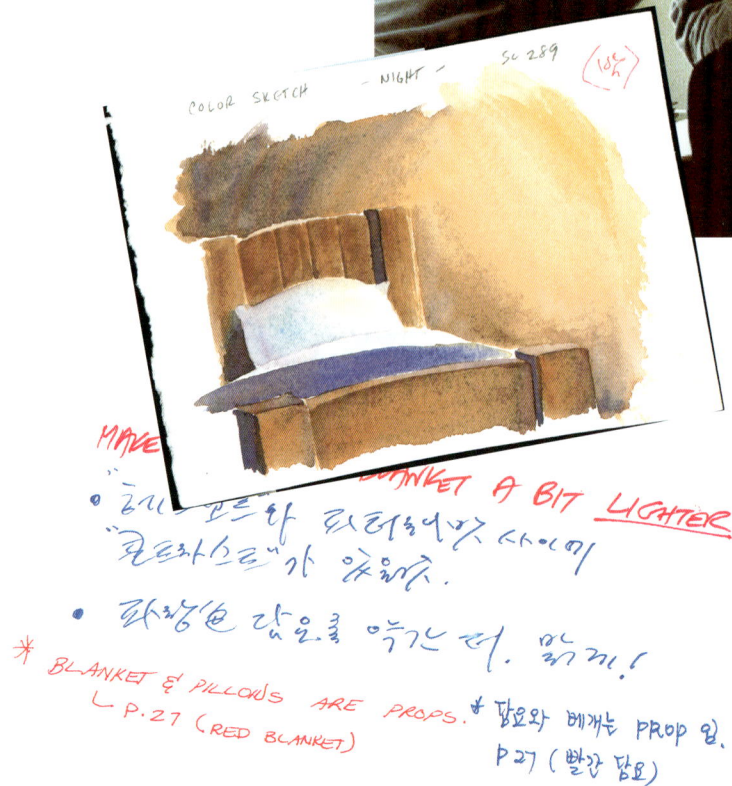

COLOR SKETCH — NIGHT — SC 289 (10ᶜ/ᵒₖ)

MAVE

· 그녀 코트와 티셔츠가 사이에
"포트라스트"가 있었죠.

· 티셔츠 담요를 약간더. 밝게!

✳ BLANKET & PILLOWS ARE PROPS. ✳ 담요와 베개는 PROP 임.
L P.27 (RED BLANKET)   P 27 (빨간 담요)

A BIT LIGHTER

Hong Kong, where customs officials insisted on opening the cans of film.

"Everything would have been lost," recalls Loubert, who pleaded with the officials to leave his precious film alone. "Finally, they opened a can in a black bag and agreed that it was just film, and I was allowed to go through."

While Smith and Loubert were in Korea trying to get *Care Bears* made, Hirsh was in the U.S. promoting the as yet non-existent movie. The producers had wanted Nelvana to screen *Care Bears* for the movie exhibitors before its release, but because the deadline was so tight, it wasn't ready to be shown.

"We had almost nothing to show them," recalls Hirsh. So he found a way to turn the problem into an advantage. He went on the road with some Leica reels (pencil sketches of the animated story arranged in sequence and put on film so they can be viewed on a movie screen) and a little bit of preliminary colour animation. Hirsh believes he was the first to show exhibitors a work in progress, something that Disney has done since. "People loved the movie anyway," he says. "I was told it was considered great salesmanship. It made the exhibitors feel that they were part of the process because they were seeing unfinished work."

Nelvana didn't have the same stake in *Care Bears* that it had had in *Rock & Rule*. The bears weren't Nelvana's characters and the whole concept was somebody else's. Moreover, it was service work, meaning that Nelvana had been paid a fee for its efforts but would not partake in the profits. So after the movie was finished, everybody got busy on other projects and forgot about *Care Bears*.

Then, on the evening of Good Friday 1985, Hirsh got a phone call from Patrick Loubert.

Loubert said, "You'll never believe this, but I just drove past a theatre that has a line around the block."

Hirsh said, "Yeah?"

"Do you know what movie it is?"

"No."

"It's the *Care Bears* movie."

They had both forgotten the film was opening that weekend. But millions of Care Bear owners hadn't forgotten. They were out in force, clutching their bears, and because pre-schoolers don't go to the movies alone, their parents were out in force as well. *Care Bears,* made for two- to four-year-olds, one of the youngest target audiences of any animated movie, became the highest-grossing non-Disney animated film to that time. And it won the Golden Reel Award that goes every year to the highest-grossing Canadian movie.

Naturally, the success of *Care Bears* caused regret among the partners that they didn't own any of it. "We could have waived our fee and taken a big piece of the film," recalls Loubert. "We were offered that deal. But if we had waived the fee, we couldn't have made the payroll. Once the picture was hugely successful, we thought we should have waived the fee. But we couldn't have."

The same Catch-22 situation confronted Nelvana's owners all through the 1980s and into the 1990s. They hadn't yet figured out that their goal should be to do only proprietary production, but they knew they should do more of it. Yet they couldn't afford to because they needed the quick cash that service work provided.

Proprietary work has higher profit margins and allows the studio to build a library of programs that keep earning money years after the cost of making them has been paid off. Moreover,

HIRSH, LOUBERT, AND SMITH IN THE SCREENING ROOM AT THEIR LAKE SHORE BOULEVARD STUDIO IN 1987 AS TWO OF THEIR YOUNG STARS LOOK ON.

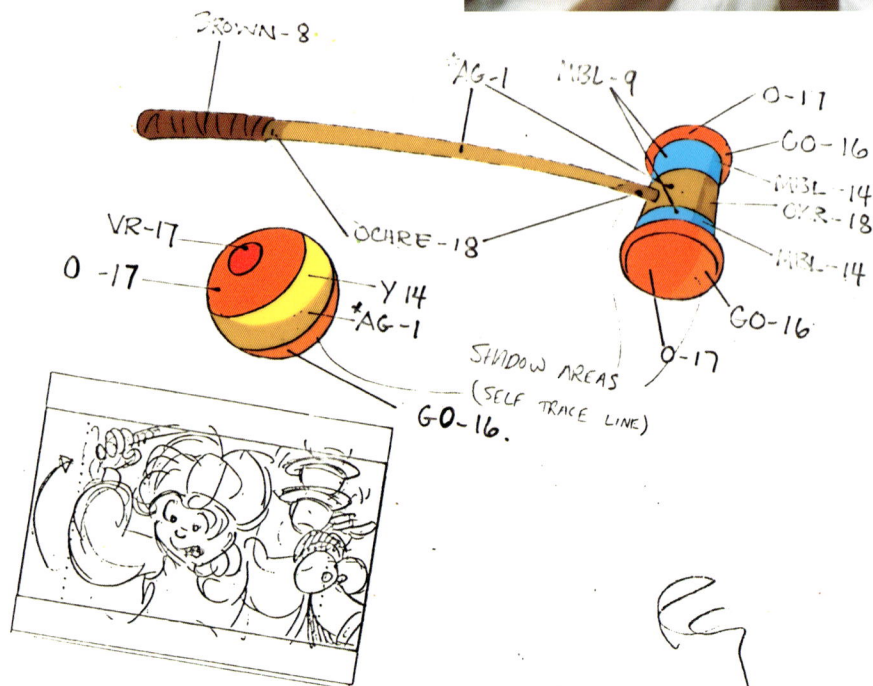

Canada copyright © 1986 Nelvana Limited
Copyright © 1986 Those Characters From Cleveland,

proprietary work keeps the creative staff happier. "Your senior people don't want to do service work," explains Loubert. "You are working for other people who may not know anything, but they know they don't like something, so they say 'Change this' for no reason. That's when your senior people go somewhere else. It's not satisfying on a professional level."

What made the situation more frustrating was that with its series of holiday specials Nelvana had long since proved it could do proprietary work successfully. "It's our strength," says Loubert. "Not everybody can do it, but we can."

Nelvana had the talent and know-how but it lacked a crucial ingredient—financial strength. John Vander-velde, who was doing Nelvana's books in those days for KPMG, a large accounting firm, knew as well as anyone how frail the company's finances were. "We wondered every year if we would be back at Nelvana because its financial situation was dire at most times," he recalls.

Vandervelde became a specialist in the entertainment industry when, looking for a way out of a dull job at IBM, he answered an advertisement for accountants to work in entertainment. "I went to the movies every couple of weeks; that's all I knew about entertainment," he recalls. "Not until I got there did I realize that if accounting firms advertise outside for people to work in a new department, it must mean it's not a good department. Nobody wanted to work in entertainment because the clients were all so small and none of them were making money."

Now Vandervelde works in-house as Nelvana's vice-president and treasurer. "I got here in 1993 and even then we used to have weekly meetings wondering how we were going to make payroll. We'd sit in the boardroom and think of customers we could chase for money."

That was the heart of the problem—getting customers to pay so that Nelvana in turn could pay its own staff. It's no wonder Loubert still has payroll nightmares: meeting the payroll is fundamental. If you can't do it, you shouldn't be in business. However, while your workers can't wait for their money, your clients think you should be willing to wait a very long time for yours. On average, now as then, it takes 18 months to get paid for a series. Suppose Nelvana does 13 episodes of a series and sells it to a German TV network. The network pays 10 per cent on signing the deal, 50 per cent when the series is delivered, and the final 40 per cent a year later. Today, the average episode costs about US$325,000 to make, which works out to around CAN$7 million for the series. Nelvana pays that upfront but has to wait 18 months for full payment.

Obviously, a company in this situation needs bridge financing, but in the 1980s, Canadian banks were just as queasy about the entertainment industry as the large accounting firms were. As a pioneer in building a Canadian film industry, part of Nelvana's job was to educate bankers. The Canadian banks didn't know anything about the industry, and because most of Nelvana's sales were foreign, they weren't familiar with its customers. "Banks like to understand who your customers and suppliers are," explains Vandervelde. "If they don't know them, they aren't going to give you value on them." Nelvana might have a piece of paper that says a German TV network will pay it $7 million for a series. But what if Nelvana doesn't deliver? What if the network doesn't pay? And what is this German network anyway? A banker with no knowledge of the industry is not going to loan much money on the basis of that piece of paper.

One day in September 1988, there was a knock on Patrick Loubert's front door. He went to open it, his daughter and son trailing behind. A man named Wayne Drury was there. He stepped back into the front yard and screamed at Loubert.

"You started shooting," he roared. "I am going to lose my job. And if I go down, you are going down. Down, down, down."

Loubert and his amazed children stood there open-mouthed as the man, having had his say, turned on his heel and departed.

At the time, Drury was the Royal Bank executive in charge of Nelvana's account and he was upset about the way Nelvana was proceeding on a live action project called T and T. Nelvana had switched its business to the Royal Bank after the CIBC had closed its Rochdale branch. Not long after, the Royal Bank decided to set up a group specializing in entertainment, headed by Drury. Despite Drury's frequent emotional outbursts, his arrival as the head of the Royal Bank's entertainment business turned out to be one of the best things ever to happen to Nelvana.

Because of Drury, who died in 1992, the Royal became the bank of the film industry, as the Toronto-Dominion is the bank of the broadcasting industry. "Wayne was the first who was convinced of the viability of the film and television business for the bank," says Loubert. "Until him, we had always had bank managers who were really lenders in other sectors. We helped educate Wayne, and Wayne helped educate the bank."

Harriet Reisman is Nelvana's senior vice-president and general counsel. In the 1980s, she worked as a lawyer for two major law firms, specializing in entertainment. One of her clients was the Royal Bank, so she worked closely with Drury. Without access to credit, the Canadian film industry could not have grown, and Drury, more than anyone else, opened up the purse strings. "Had it not been for Wayne and his initiative with the Royal Bank, the industry would not have developed as it did," Reisman says.

In those days, each production was financed separately, so the bank had to inform itself about each deal and all the players in it. Before Reisman started working with him, Drury had employed a Los Angeles lawyer, who taught him a lot about evaluating the collateral of film companies. The key issues are whether the studio will deliver and whether the broadcaster will pay. The more the banker knows, the more confidently he or she can answer these questions. But the banker can't just make the loan and put the file away; he or she has to keep track of what's going on. The banker has to know the production schedules and whether or not things are going smoothly. And Drury had to get involved not just with his own client but with the client's customer as well; before approving credit, he would make a network agree not to change the contract date unilaterally or reduce the licence fee.

Drury also did business with other film companies, including Atlantis, Alliance, Paragon, and Telescene. "Wayne on many occasions saved companies from having to shut down

(OPPOSITE PAGE) THE CARE BEARS ADVENTURE IN WONDERLAND. (BELOW) LITTLE ROSEY WAS DEVELOPED WITH ROSEANNE BARR.

and not make payroll," recounts Reisman. "And if the production had not been made, would you have the credibility to hire the people for the next production?"

The screaming fit at Loubert's front door was not an isolated incident. "Wayne was always there for his clients but he made their lives hell along the way," says Reisman. "He'd use me to send horrible messages but he did a lot of his own dirty work. He'd say: 'We're shutting this down.' Or, 'If you've got your house on the line, that's too bad.' He was practically abusive. But he wanted to make sure they were doing everything they could to hold up their piece of the bargain. He wanted to keep the pressure on them.

"And what the clients didn't know was that while he was being abusive to them he was also abusive to senior people at the bank. He'd say: 'Get

your head out of the sand, this is where the world is going. Look at Hollywood. We've got to develop our own thing.'

"The senior people were skeptical," Reisman recalls. "Their attitude was that he was exposing the bank to risk and it was because he had stars in his eyes. He brought the bank into an industry that was in its infancy. It was high risk and his credibility was on the line. The bank stood to lose lots of money, and if somebody's head was going to roll, you could be sure it was his."

In the case of Paragon, the bank did lose money, but the percentage of bad loans for the industry as a whole is lower than average. "In most cases, it's a licence to print money for the banks," says Vandervelde. "All of Nelvana's customers are big media companies, half of them are state-owned, so they're not much of a credit risk. You rarely get stiffed."

Still, it wasn't until the 1990s that Nelvana finally was able to establish itself on solid financial footing. For most of the 1980s, recalls Michael Harrison, the company "was on the edge every month. At one point, I went to the Royal Bank and put my signature on a note so that we could meet the payroll. But the company always met the bills, it always got everything paid. And the quality of the product started to show."

Inspector Gadget had taught Nelvana an important lesson. "We decided that making series was where the money was," says Loubert. Since a lot of work goes into developing characters and an environment for the characters to live in, it's more profitable to exploit that material in a series of programs rather than in just one.

Loubert explains: "Once you've got one program, you can make two, three, and four. The second is not as hard as the first, the third is not as hard as the second, and the fourth is not as hard as the third. Within a certain set of parameters, you don't change a lot once you get that first one."

So the rest of the 1980s was devoted to establishing Nelvana as an efficient producer of television series. In 1984, it launched *The Edison Twins*, its first live action series, a co-production with CBC and the Disney Channel. Michael Hirsh, with his lifelong interest in science, came up with the idea of a program based on kids having adventures in which they use scientific inventions to solve the problem. Nelvana made 78 half-hour episodes before production ended in 1986. The show, owned by Nelvana, is still seen in reruns.

Another live action series was *T and T*, of which 65 episodes were made between 1987 and 1989. The show starred former professional wrestler Mr. T in the role of T.S. Turner, an ex-boxer turned private detective. This project almost caused a financial disaster for Nelvana, through no fault of its own. A U.S. company called Quintex was the holding company for the distribution entity that was distributing *T and T.* Quintex was paying Nelvana weekly advances that, along with credit advanced by the Royal Bank, were being used to

MOTION PICTURE GUARANTORS LTD.
Congratulates
cast and crew
on the successful on time, on budget
completion and delivery of

"T and T" Series III

Executive Producers - Patrick Loubert
Clive Smith
Michael Hirsh
Producer - John Ryan

CINÉGARANTIE LTÉE · MOTION PICTURE GUARANTORS LTD.

(LEFT) TO ENSURE THAT THE T AND T SERIES CAME IN ON TIME AND ON BUDGET, LOUBERT DIRECTED THE FINAL THREE EPISODES HIMSELF AND SHOT THEM SIMULTANEOUSLY IN THREE DAYS.
(BELOW) THE EDISON TWINS (PLAYED BY ANDREW SABISTON AND MARNIE MCPHAIL), ALONG WITH THEIR YOUNGER BROTHER (PLAYED BY SUNNY THRASHER), DREW UPON THEIR KNOWLEDGE OF SCIENCE TO SOLVE MYSTERIES EACH WEEK.

or three projects at any one time. In 1988, *T and T* was the most important project it had going. With Quintex bankrupt, not only would Nelvana not have the money it needed to finish making the series but there might be no way of distributing it even if it were completed. Five years after the *Rock & Rule* debacle, Nelvana once again seemed to be on the brink of doom.

Michael Hirsh was on a sales trip in Europe, where it was 1 a.m., when Loubert called him at his hotel.

"Michael, we have a real problem. Quintex has gone bankrupt."

Hirsh mumbled, "OK, I'll talk to you in the morning."

Hirsh's low-key reaction reassured Loubert. Maybe it's not as bad as I thought, he said to himself. But five minutes later his phone rang. Hirsh was on the line and he was shouting: "Did you just phone and tell me Quintex is bankrupt? We're totally screwed. This is terrible."

Hirsh, a deep sleeper, had imagined that Loubert's call had been a bad dream. But the nightmare was all too real. Somehow, Nelvana had to extract *T and T* from the Quintex bankruptcy, get the show back in production, resell it, and refinance it. The problem was that when a company goes bankrupt, both it and its creditors are focussed on the big picture, not on one asset.

finance production. One evening at 7 p.m., Loubert's phone rang. A lawyer for Quintex was on the line.

The lawyer said, "I've got 15 people in the room. Do you want to be introduced to them?"

Loubert said, "What's this about?"

The lawyer said, "There's a problem here. Quintex is bankrupt. This is a bankruptcy forum in which we are phoning all of the active units to inform them of the situation."

If something of the kind happened today, when Nelvana has 23 series in production, it would be a problem, but it would not put the company's existence in jeopardy. But in the 1980s, Nelvana usually had only two

T and T meant little to Quintex or the creditors but it meant everything to Nelvana. If Nelvana couldn't rescue *T and T,* it too would go bankrupt.

Eleanor Olmsted, Nelvana's general counsel, had to get *T and T* out of the bankruptcy proceedings. This was difficult to do because normally all assets are dealt with in court at the same time. But her argument was a strong one—unless the *T and T* situation was resolved immediately, that particular asset would never be worth anything to anybody. Moreover, Quintex managers didn't want to see its own bankruptcy cause Nelvana to go under as well. So Nelvana was able to acquire both the show and its distribution rights. A process that could have taken years had taken two weeks.

The next step was to refinance the show. Drury took care of that by putting up some more of the Royal Bank's money. That set the stage for the banker's unannounced visit to Loubert's house. Drury was angry because Loubert had started shooting before Drury had the contracts he needed to release the cash flow. But Loubert felt he had no choice: "If I had waited any longer, we would have either lost Mr. T or not finished by Christmas, which was our deadline. After he finished screaming, he got in his car and left. But he put the payroll through."

Loubert stepped in and directed some of the final *T and T* episodes himself. It was his last experience as a director. Because of his duties managing a growing company, he no longer has time to direct, something he regrets. Photographs of him on the *T and T* set adorn his office wall. "It was a terrible time but we got through it, and the series is still playing in reruns," he says.

To survive, grow, and prosper, companies need to be adept at responding to adversity. Nelvana had

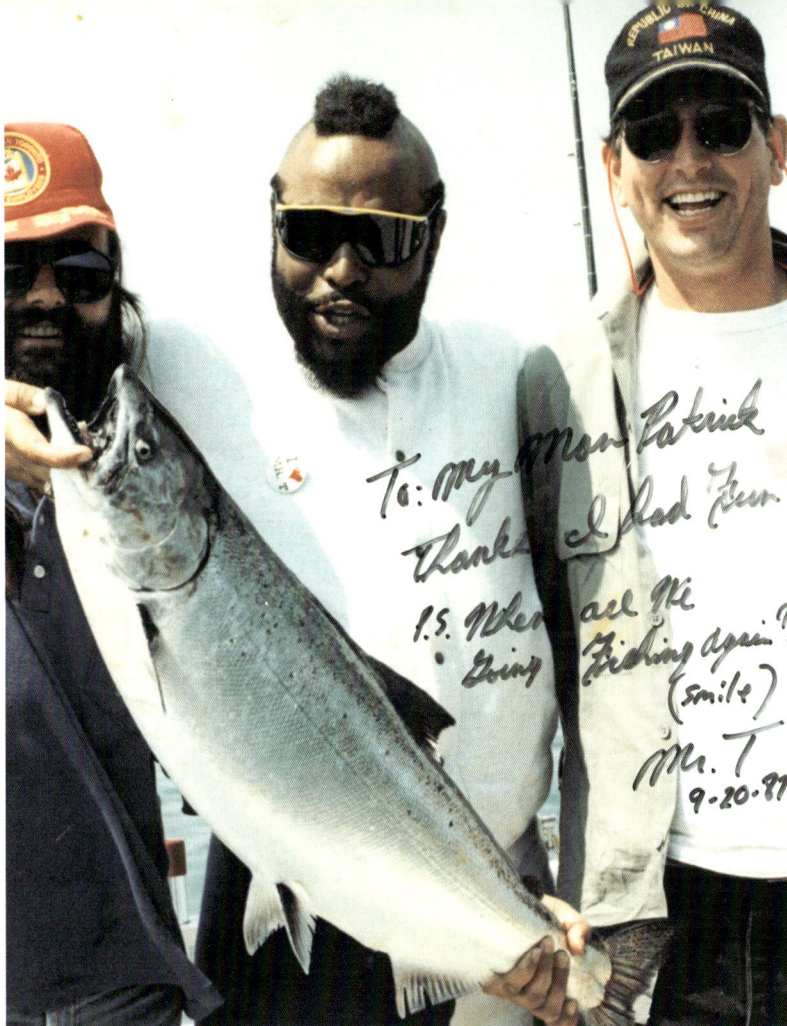

To: my Mom Patrick
Thanks I had fun
P.S. When are We
Going Fishing again?
(smile)
Mr. T
9-20-89

(LEFT) LOUBERT AND MR. T ON A FISHING TRIP. (BELOW) ELEANOR OLMSTED WAS GENERAL COUNSEL FOR NELVANA FOR MANY YEARS.

Beetlejuice© 1989 The Geffen Company

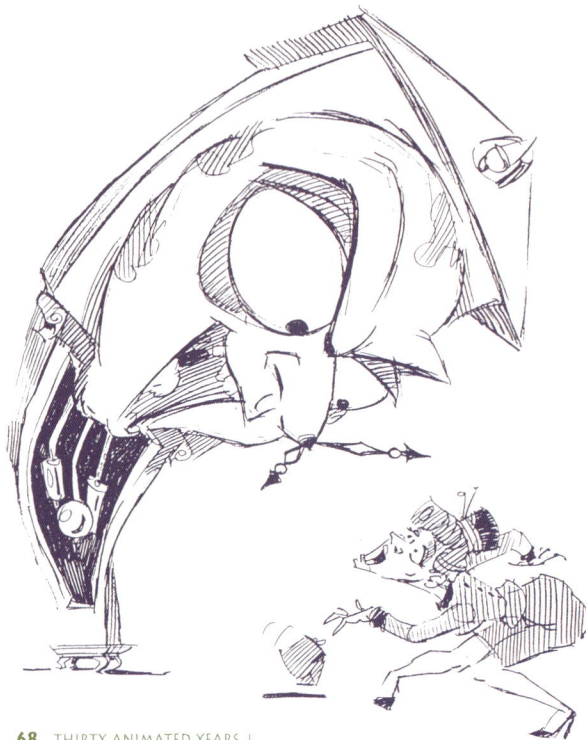

done that once in the case of *Rock & Rule* and now it had done it again.

The strategy adopted after *Rock & Rule*—becoming a volume producer in order to get out of debt—was working. As the decade wound down, most of the debt was retired. While an emphasis on service work was not a good long-term strategy for Nelvana, it had served an important financial purpose during the 1980s and, in some cases, had been interesting from an artistic perspective as well. For example, when George Lucas had wanted to do two 13-episode TV series, *Droids* and *Ewoks*, based on *Star Wars*, he had called Nelvana. *Droids* was a show about the adventures of R2-D2 and C-3P0 before they joined Luke Skywalker. *Ewoks* was about the teddy bears of the same name who appeared in the third *Star Wars* movie.

As in Nelvana's previous collaboration with Lucas, there was resistance from the U.S. network that was to broadcast the shows. "There was a huge problem convincing ABC that we were the producers that should be making the shows," recalls Hirsh. "They wanted L.A. guys."

They had to settle for Toronto guys instead. This was a big step forward for Nelvana, and not just because it sent more badly needed

cash flowing into the company's bank account. "Because of *Droids* and *Ewoks*, we broke in as network suppliers," explains Hirsh. And because Nelvana was accepted as an important supplier to networks around the world, it eventually became the successful business it is today.

Working for Lucas was always a stimulating, creative experience. There were many conversations with him about such subjects as how to tell a story and the importance of fairy tales. Smith remembers one scene in particular, in which R2-D2 is in a ship that explodes. He manages to escape, and the viewer sees him afterward in a parachute. That wasn't good enough for Lucas. He wanted the figure of R2-D2 escaping as the explosion took place even though he wouldn't be visible to the viewer if the film were shown at normal speed. "The audience wouldn't be able to see him, but he had to be in there. Those are the kinds of details that George would insist on," says Smith.

Another exciting service job was *Beetlejuice*, an animated series made in 1989 based on the live action Tim Burton movie of the same name made the year before. Clive Smith hugely enjoyed working with Burton, whose quirky style and off-the-wall sense of humour resembled his own. With

Beetlejuice, Nelvana was developing a skill that would be one of the foundations of its success in the 1990s—the ability to adapt the creative visions of others without losing the essence of the original.

Meanwhile, the spectacular success of *Care Bears* had helped revive the whole market for young children's entertainment, and Nelvana moved to take advantage of the opportunity it had helped to create. It acquired the movie and TV rights to the popular bears and produced a second movie, *The Care Bears Adventure in Wonderland,* released in 1987, as well as a *Care Bears* television series. Produced between 1986 and 1988, it ran for 52 episodes and was broadcast in 140 countries.

If you were a small child in the 1950s and your parents read books to you, one of the books would almost certainly have been *The Story of Babar,* by Jean de Brunhoff. It is the story of an elephant who, after a hunter kills his mother, goes to the city, acquires a stylish wardrobe, marries his cousin Céleste, and returns to become king of the elephants. This book and five others written during the 1930s by de Brunhoff, a French writer and painter, are among the best-loved classics of children's literature.

(LEFT) LOUBERT, HIRSH, AND SMITH AT A PRESS VIEWING OF BABAR ART, WITH LAURENT DE BRUNHOFF AND HIS WIFE, PHYLLIS ROSE.
(BELOW) KING BABAR AND QUEEN CÉLESTE.

Michael Hirsh's earliest literary memories are of being read the Babar stories, in their original French, by his francophone parents. "It's indelibly fixed in my mind," he says. When he was a young child in Toronto, his family lived a short walk from the building housing the Osborne collection of the Toronto Public Library. It was one of the best children's libraries in the world, and Hirsh was taken there often to hear story readings. "I'm sure I heard Babar being read there as well," he says.

In 1985, Kevin McCormick, who was then running Nelvana's Los Angeles office, attended a dinner party at which he met Clifford Ross, who was in negotiations with de Brunhoff's son, Laurent, to acquire the entertainment and merchandising rights for Babar. When Hirsh heard about this, he was immediately interested. He started discussions that eventually led to Nelvana getting the rights to bring Babar to life on the screen.

Just because a character from a book is venerable and famous—and Babar was both—doesn't mean it is an automatic candidate for a successful movie or TV show.

In fact, Nelvana's decision to adapt Babar was a risky and audacious one. De Brunhoff's stories had been around for 50 years and nobody had ever tried to make a series based on them. If Nelvana went ahead, it would have to write its own stories because the existing ones did not contain enough action to sustain a movie or a TV series. Moreover, a Babar movie or TV show would be subjected to more critical scrutiny than a show based on, say, the Care Bears. Those were just commercial products, but Babar was a character that had enthralled generations of children. Many of those children were now parents who would not support a movie that took liberties with him.

Those were the least of the problems. More serious was that Nelvana's key market, the U.S., was not receptive to foreign literary properties. American kids loved the Babar books but American broadcasters, Hirsh soon found out, didn't. Not only was Babar foreign but his appeal was to the under-four audience—a demographic group that didn't have great appeal to advertisers since its members are too young to make their own purchasing decisions.

Not only was the U.S. cool to the idea of a screen version of Babar, so was Babar's native France, recounts Emmanuèle Petry, the Paris-based vice-president of Nelvana International Ltd. "At the time, in France, Babar was kind of old-fashioned," she says. "It was not at all what kids were looking at. When I was a kid, we watched Babar on TV as puppets. It was only a five-minute program and it was very slow and boring. Nobody had ever thought of making a series.

"But Michael really believed in it. He was probably one of the only ones. He persuaded Canal Plus [a French network] to co-produce it and it was a big risk for them because it was considered one of those old-fashioned, dusty properties. It was Michael's genius to believe in it and persuade everybody to put a lot of money into it. That's his nose, as we say in French. He has a good nose."

Obviously, the elephant has a place in Hirsh's heart, but Nelvana launched its Babar project for business reasons, not sentimental ones. It needed to reduce its dependency on the U.S. market, and doing the Babar project was a good way to start. To that point, Nelvana had relied on the three major U.S. networks. One year it might have three or four shows on TV but the next year it might sell only one. So the company's business, including the size of its staff, was constantly shrinking and expanding.

(OPPOSITE PAGE) TIN TIN WAS A MUCH-LOVED COMIC-BOOK CHARACTER BEFORE BEING TRANSFORMED INTO THE HERO OF A TELEVISION SERIES.
(LEFT) EMMANUÈLE PETRY, VICE-PRESIDENT OF NELVANA ENTERPRISES AND DIRECTOR OF SALES FOR EUROPE, SHARES THE PARIS OFFICE WITH PATRICIA BURNS AND A SMALL DEVELOPMENT AND SALES STAFF.
(BELOW) KING BABAR AND HIS COURTIERS.

"Babar came in a year when we were disappointed in the number of series we had sold," Hirsh says. "It was down from the previous year. By doing Babar as a foreign co-production we had more control of our destiny. We were no longer relying on three U.S. buyers." Moving into non–North American markets in a big way was a crucial step for Nelvana. Today, these markets deliver the largest share of the company's revenues.

Babar: The Movie came out in 1989, and 65 half-hour TV episodes started airing in the same year. A second movie, *Babar: King of the Elephants*, appeared in 1998, and a new set of 13 episodes was produced in 2000 and 2001. The original Babar series was broadcast in 150 countries. Despite the initial reluctance of American buyers, those countries included the U.S., because a U.S. cable channel, Home Box Office (HBO), bought the series once Nelvana had begun production. Adding a cable network to its client list was another positive step toward stability. The on-air networks all wanted shows delivered in September, which meant Nelvana had to organize its workforce to get all its productions ready at the same time. Cable networks, on the other hand, will accept delivery at other times of the year, which enabled the studio to space out the work and offer year-long employment to more people.

The Babar project was pivotal for Nelvana; it enabled the company to find its true vocation. "Starting with Babar, we developed an expertise in bringing great books to life," explains Hirsh. "The company was more than halfway through its life when we discovered that this is perhaps what we do best." Adapting a famous literary property has business advantages as well. While Nelvana still creates its own original projects with its own original characters, it is easier to sell an already famous character or a new project from a well-known author.

In making an adaptation, the filmmakers inevitably have to change the book to make it work in the new medium, but they have to do so without losing whatever it was that gave the book its appeal. "We have to identify the basic values that make the characters popular," Hirsh explains. "And we build the storytelling around those values. The execution is tough because people have an expectation of what these characters do, but you have to give more than what they have done before."

The first, and most important step, is to gain the trust of the author. In this case it was Laurent de

Brunhoff, who had continued the Babar series after his father's death. Hirsh thought, and de Brunhoff agreed, that Babar should be portrayed as a father telling stories to his own children, a format that other animation companies later copied for other series. Using that format, Nelvana people, including writer Peter Sauder and directors Ray Jafelice and Dale Schott, came up with story ideas, which they presented to de Brunhoff.

Some ideas never got as far as de Brunhoff. Sauder, who is brilliant at adapting classics, remembers one that didn't make the cut. He had the notion of combining elements of *It's a Wonderful Life* and *Les Misérables* into a Babar story. In *It's a Wonderful Life*, the character played by Jimmy Stewart gets into trouble, considers suicide, and then has a dream of a terrible alternate world in which he doesn't exist. Sauder's idea was to have Babar fall asleep and have a nightmare of a *Les Misérables*-type world in which the rhinoceroses have taken over.

He took the idea to Schott, who said, "This isn't Babar. We don't want kids bawling their eyes out."

Sauder said, "What do you know? I'm the guy who knows Babar."

So Sauder presented the idea to CBC producer Debbie Bernstein.

She said, "This isn't Babar."

He got the message and changed the story to a comedy. Instead of how horrible it would be if Babar weren't king, it was about how wacky it would be if Retaxas were king instead of Babar.

Sauder says de Brunhoff has never rejected an idea that was presented to him for the TV series, but that doesn't mean Nelvana has carte blanche to do what it wants with the character. On one occasion, someone in the company broached the idea of a movie in which Babar goes to the United Nations and makes a speech about world peace. De Brunhoff rejected it. "He said it wasn't Babar," says Sauder, "and he was right."

Once the author is onside, the long, delicate process of transferring the book to the screen begins. "The printed page is a whole different thing than an animated program," says Clive Smith. "But it's our obligation to be as true to the books as possible. Babar is probably 80 per cent authentic and 20 per cent adaptation.

"Even though the animation is 2-D, animators have to think of the characters as being three-dimensional. They have to turn, they have to have a structural integrity. When you look at Jean de Brunhoff's original drawings, they are very flat, it's a two-dimensional design. It was a challenge to keep the spirit of that, the softness,

(LEFT) POST-IT NOTES AS BOARD PANELS. (BELOW) FILM AND MAGNETIC RECORDING STOCK, ONCE THE MAINSTAY OF PRE- AND POST-PRODUCTION, ARE NEARING THE END OF THEIR USEFULNESS IN THE TELEVISION INDUSTRY.

the graphic quality of the character, which was so successful in the book, and to pull out of that a structure that can turn and walk and emote.

"Most of the emotion that you read in a person is in the eyes. The laughter, the sorrow, everything is in the eyes. Babar has two little dots for eyes. So you've got to find ways of expressing emotion for a character with two little dots for eyes and a huge trunk. There are different ways to do that. You can cheat a little in the design. You can give the character an eyebrow, and you don't need to keep it there. You do it with body language. And

you do it with dialogue performance."

Casting the right actors to voice the characters is a critical step. When Smith was starting out as an animation director, he liked to sit in the studio and have fun with the actors auditioning for voice parts. Then he discovered that some of the performances he thought he liked best sounded the worst when he listened to them on tape. He had been fooled by the facial expressions and gestures of the actors. Now he won't even look at a performer during an audition.

"When you isolate the voice, that voice has to carry all those facial expressions and body language. You have to see the smile, you have to see the tears. You have to hear the shape of the performance. It is so critical," says Smith. After much deliberation, Canadian actor Gordon Pinsent was chosen for the voice of Babar.

Babar was not a Ninja Turtles–style megahit but it was a successful and much admired show and it consolidated Nelvana's reputation throughout the industry as a quality producer. In France, the video of the movie was a huge success, selling more than one million copies.

Merchandising of Babar dolls and other products was also successful in France and elsewhere. The merchandising rights are jointly licensed by

Nelvana and The Clifford Ross Company Ltd. Before Nelvana's involvement, Babar merchandising had never made more than $75,000 a year; today it earns in the millions.

However, the TV show's ratings in France were disappointing and the reasons help illustrate just how tricky it is to create programs for children. "The stories aim a little bit too high," explains Petry. "The core target is probably two to four. Kids older than four say it's a baby show. But the stories are actually very sophisticated for the two to four group. The new series is aimed more toward younger kids, and I think that will help relaunch it."

Petry sold Babar to all the major public networks in Europe. The only territory where she failed at first to make a sale was Turkey. The head of acquisitions of Turkey's major network was a bright young woman who told Petry that she loved the show but couldn't buy it.

"Why not?" Petry asked.

"It's too tender and sweet. Only violent shows work here. Couldn't you put some weapons in it? Maybe some knives?"

Well, no. That wouldn't have been Babar. Nevertheless, once the show was a hit in other countries, the Turkish network bought it despite the absence of weapons.

Nelvana's interest in Babar was a result of Michael Hirsh's childhood memories. By the time the show was produced and on the air all over the world, the partners realized they had discovered a formula that, properly implemented, could bring them long-term success. "Babar gave us a pattern," explains Loubert. "We could then look for other great characters, identify what was timeless, and go on from there. It became an important economic strategy for us too. We own the entertainment rights and we share merchandising rights with Clifford Ross."

During the 1990s, the Babar formula would be applied to other great characters from several countries, including Canada's Franklin, Sweden's Pippi Longstocking, and Britain's Rupert.

In October of 1989, Lord Stevens of Ludgate, chairman of Express Newspapers in London, received a letter that began: "I have just learned, to my dismay and outrage, that the *Daily Express* has sold the film rights to Rupert to Nelvina [sic], a Canadian animation company."

The writer was Paul, the former Beatle. Nelvina, Nelvana—whatever the Canadian company was called, McCartney was convinced that it had

no business owning the rights to so quintessentially British a bear as Rupert. The comic strip featuring Rupert is as British as fish and chips and warm beer. It has appeared in the *Express* every day since November 1920, when it was invented by Mary Tourtel, the wife of the paper's news editor. Every year, the *Express* publishes a Rupert annual that sells as many as 200,000 copies and is sent to British expatriates all over the world by their relatives back home. Prince Charles is a Rupert fan as is Paul McCartney. McCartney has gone on stage dressed like Rupert, in checked pants, red sweater, and scarf.

The musician had, as he went on to explain in his letter, been working for 20 years trying to develop Rupert into "the greatest British animated film." Not only that, Sir Max Aitken, a previous chairman of Express Newspapers, "had promised me that, unlike what happened to Winnie the Pooh, Rupert would always remain British." (The rights to Winnie the Pooh are owned by Disney.)

In 1984, McCartney had made a short movie called *Rupert and the Frog Song*, which became a best-selling video. A song he performed in the video, *We All Stand Together*, was also

NELVANA PRODUCED
65 EPISODES FEATURING RUPERT.

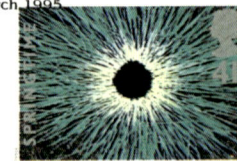

Benham, Folkestone, Kent (Benham) BLCS102

a hit. So why, the letter concluded, would the *Express* now assign the film rights to someone else?

McCartney wasn't the only one asking that question. A rival newspaper printed a cartoon of Rupert on a skateboard with a Walkman and earphones as a parody of how North Americans would debase the dignified British bear. But Stevens was in no mood to back down. He pointed out in his reply that McCartney's rights to Rupert had lapsed in 1984 and had not been renewed. While the singer had talked about doing a Rupert film for many

years, negotiations between him and the *Express* had not resulted in a deal. "Nelvana do, we believe, have a proven track record in terms of film, TV, and character merchandising ... We at the *Express* believe that Nelvana is capable of achieving production in the near future and maximizing that potential to the general benefit of Rupert and the *Express*."

Hirsh believes McCartney was convinced the *Express* wouldn't dare take Rupert away from him: "They negotiated a deal with us and they let his lawyers know that they were going to turn to this other deal unless they heard from him. He never contacted them. Then they sent him notice that

they had entered into a deal with Nelvana. He got very upset and took it personally."

McCartney has since rejected several offers from Nelvana to become involved in Rupert projects. Meanwhile, Nelvana has lived up to its part of the bargain. Hirsh explains: "The sales pitch that got us Rupert was that we had a good track record of taking projects and getting them made. I told the *Daily Express* that we would get it made within 12 months if we got it and we did. We got a series sold into the U.K. and Canada. We made 65 half-hours for TV, we've developed a Rupert movie, and we will make more TV shows."

Nelvana started the 1980s by venturing into Paul McCartney's territory—rock and roll—with a musical feature, *Rock & Rule*, that left it virtually bankrupt. Perhaps it was fitting that it ended the decade by taking a project in its territory—animation for children—away from one of the wealthiest and most powerful rock musicians in the world.

At the beginning of the 1980s, Nelvana's ambition was to be a major film studio but it didn't know how to go about it. By the end of the 1980s, it had almost figured that out. It knew that it had a gift for adapting great literary characters to the screen. It knew that series were more profitable than specials and that proprietary production was better than service work. It also knew that, inviting as the U.S. market was, it needed to go farther afield and that doing international co-productions was better than trying to go it alone. Nelvana hadn't yet fully understood the significance of all these elements, nor was its business organized well enough to take full advantage of what it had learned and of the talents of its people. But it had come a long way in one decade.

FROM TIN TIN.

THE MAKING OF LITTLE BEAR

Little Bear seems like a simple, quiet show: the adventures of a young bear as he makes his way in the world. It's aimed at pre-schoolers and contains no violence or mayhem. An episode consists of three separate stories, each lasting about eight minutes. Most of the stories deal with problems that a small child can identify with—not knowing where a stuffed toy is, for example, and learning, with the help of his kind and patient mother, how to go about finding it.

And yet, while the stories in *Little Bear* may be simple, the making of a *Little Bear* story is anything but. Each installment takes six months to create, from the time a Nelvana writer starts work on a script until it's ready to go on air. As many as 200 people may be involved in the creation of one three-part episode of *Little Bear*. The credits at the end of a typical program name 12 storyboard artists, 18 layout artists, 44 digital painters, 29 voice talents, and many, many more. The list would be longer if it included the artists in Korea who do most of the animation.

Like any TV show or movie, it all starts with the script. Nelvana's specialty is faithfully rendering the works of great children's authors into cinematic form. Faithfulness requires collaboration with the creators of the original works—in the case of *Little Bear*, artist Maurice Sendak and writer Else Holmelund Minarik. Nelvana's strategy is to assign a key creative person on its staff to be the chief liaison between the company and the original creators. Ray Jafelice, one of the company's most experienced artists and directors, took on this task for the *Little Bear* project.

The collaboration is more intense at the beginning stages of a project. That's the stage at which the two sides are getting to know each other. "Else Minarik and Maurice would reject certain ideas if they didn't have the right feel," recalls Jafelice. "Maurice always says avoid the cliché. He likes little twists. It's a very safe world that Little Bear is in, but there are sharp corners that you can bump your knee on."

Eventually, the rejected script ideas are fewer and fewer. "You need to make the author comfortable," says Jafelice. "It's a big help if the author understands that the show has to evolve. It must be sort of like having children: at one point they grow up and they have to go their own way and you have to let go."

Adapting a novel for adults into a screenplay is, in large part, a process of deciding what events to leave out. Adapting a story for pre-schoolers to the TV screen is the opposite—the big issue for the writer is what to add, as not much happens in most stories for pre-schoolers.

"The books are very simple," says Jafelice. "They are learn-to-read books. There isn't much plot, but there is lots of character there. As long as you maintain the characters and the richness of the characters comes out, you can get away with simpler stories.

Jafelice insists that the visual takes precedence over the verbal in the scripts for *Little Bear*. "Just as the words in a picture book are there mainly to support the images and be a tool for children to learn what words mean, so should dialogue be used to support the images in a TV show as well as strengthen the characters," he says. "Many of today's cartoons suffer from the 'talking heads' syndrome. There's too much yakking going on. If you need that much dialogue to explain your story, you don't have a strong story."

Once the script is approved, the program goes into production. Early production work is done at Nelvana's Toronto headquarters; the in-betweening, ink and paint is done in Korea; and the post-production is done in Toronto, where all the elements are put together to make the finished product.

The first step in pre-production is to create a storyboard, a visual script that details the staging of the action from scene to scene. For *Little Bear*, the storyboard for each eight-minute story requires from 200 to 300 sketches.

Next comes the recording session in which actors deliver the dialogue that the scriptwriter has created. As with the scripts in the early stages of the *Little Bear* project, the creators were also involved in choosing the key voices. Jafelice and his team selected the ones they liked best and sent them to the creators in the U.S. for their feedback. The actor chosen in 1995 to do the most important voice in the show, Little Bear himself, was an 11-year-old girl named Kristin Fairlie.

Fairlie was one of many who auditioned for the part. As an 11-year-old, the voice came naturally to her. "It was the voice I came up with and it pretty much just sounded like me," she says. "As I got older, it was a little difficult. I started listening to tapes before I went for sessions. But I would say the voice is almost exactly the same as when I started doing it."

When Fairlie was just starting the role, Jafelice and voice director Dan Hennessey used to give her the same advice, words of wisdom she has never forgotten: "The thing they said to me most often was, 'Remember, you're furry and low to the ground.'"

In a recording session, the actors, working under the supervision of the voice director, deliver their lines. "Sometimes the whole cast records together," Fairlie says. "But because Little Bear talks to himself a lot, often it's just me in there."

The actors have to stand still when recording lest the noise of rustling clothes make its way to the soundtrack. Those less experienced in voice work also have to learn that their characters, even though they will be drawn, are real. "There is a tendency in animation to do cartoon voices," says Jafelice. "I tell them, 'I just want to hear your own voice, please.' What it does is it makes them act instead of doing some cliché thing."

The voices are then broken down syllable by syllable for the animators to follow. There is a lip-synch chart in which a certain shape of the mouth represents a particular vowel or consonant. An "exposure sheet" that lists every frame of film is created. In this, every word used is spelled phonetically with the chart for the Korean animators who don't speak English.

The layout department, working from the storyboard, prepares a layout that separates the various elements of a scene, including background, animation, poses, props, overlays, and camera instructions.

For each episode, 20 to 30 in-betweeners in Korea complete the scenes on paper, and other artists paint the backgrounds which were designed in Toronto. A film running at normal speed contains 24 frames per second. In *Little Bear*, every second frame is a new drawing, so there are 12 drawings per second and 17,280 drawings for each 24-minute program.

The animation is then scanned into a computer, put on tape, and shipped back to Toronto, where the post-production takes place. In the past, the artwork was filmed by cameras. Now computers are used to do the final composition in which the voice and artwork is melded into a finished show.

Ray Jafelice has worked at Nelvana for 22 years and was instrumental in creating the *Babar* series and films. "It's a special treat to work with people like Maurice Sendak and Laurent de Brunhoff, whom I have admired for a long time," he says.

There's also a lot of satisfaction in working on a long-running show because of the camaraderie that develops among the actors who perform the voices.

But the most satisfying thing of all is to know that your work brings pleasure to countless children in the 131 countries where *Little Bear* is shown on television.

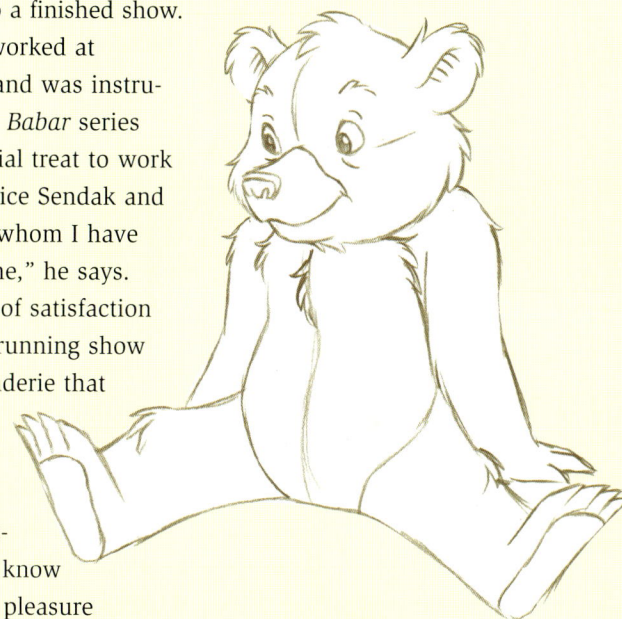

IN 1987, NELVANA INCORPORATED
BEARSPOTS, A COMPANY SPECIALIZING
IN COMMERCIALS. ITS LOGO WAS THE
NELVANA BEAR WITH SPOTS, THE INDUSTRY
TERM FOR COMMERCIALS.
BEARSPOTS PRODUCED COMMERCIALS
FOR SUCH MAJOR COMPANIES AS NABISCO,
TOYOTA, PLANTERS AND PILLSBURY.
IT ALSO PRODUCED THE FIRST OMNIMAX
ANIMATION FOR A PROJECT FOR EXPO '95
AND A FULLY ANIMATED VIDEO GAME
FOR VIRGIN INTERACTIVE CALLED
TOONSTRUCK. THE DIVISION EMPLOYED UP
TO 40 PEOPLE AND ALSO BORROWED
THE TALENTS OF NELVANA ANIMATORS
FROM MAINSTREAM PRODUCTION. BUT BY
1995, NELVANA HAD DECIDED TO
ELIMINATE CONTRACT WORK AND TO FOCUS
ON PROPRIETORY PRODUCTION.
AS A RESULT, IT CLOSED BEARSPOTS.

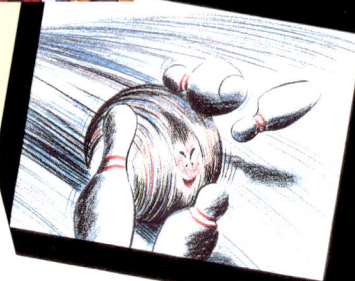

BEAR·SPOTS
ANIMATION FOR EVERYONE!
BEAR·SPOTS
30 ATLANTIC AVE.
TORONTO, ONT, M6K 1X8
(416)588-8555
(416)588-5252
CALL NORM... OR CLIVE
A NELVANA COMPANY
ALSO AT
9000 Sunset Blvd, Los Angeles, CA 90069
466 Fax: (213) 278-4872

BEAR·SPOTS

CLIVE A. SMITH
President and Creative Director
30 ATLANTIC AVE., TORONTO, ONTARIO, CANADA M6K 1X8 (416) 588-8555 (416) 588-5252
9000 SUNSET BLVD., LOS ANGELES, CA. 90069 (213) 278-8460 (213) 278-4872

A NELVANA COMPANY

Cycle Safely
"Road Warrior"
30 Sec. English
Kert Advertising
Toronto City Cycling Committee
Fully Rendered in Colour Pencil
Continuous Animation Throughout

IT GOES BEYOND THE THRILL OF SEEING THE BOOK CHARACTERS COME TO LIFE.
THE TEAMS AT NELVANA HAVE EMBRACED FRANKLIN. THERE IS A RESPECT FOR HIS PAST AND
FAITH IN HIS FUTURE.

BRENDA CLARK, ILLUSTRATOR OF FRANKLIN

I WAS WATCHING THE FIRST TELEVISED EPISODE OF FRANKLIN WITH MY TEENAGE CHILDREN
AND THEIR FRIENDS. WHEN SNAIL STARTED TO SOB, EVERY ONE OF THEM WIPED AWAY A TEAR.
THEY WERE GENUINELY TOUCHED BY THE DEPTH OF HIS EXPRESSION. THE ANIMATION HAS
MADE WOODLAND FEEL LIKE A REAL PLACE.

PAULETTE BOURGEOIS, CREATOR OF FRANKLIN

FEW PEOPLE HAVE THE CHANCE TO LEARN SOMETHING SOUP TO NUTS WHEN THEY ARE
IN THEIR LATE 50s. IN THE SHORT TIME WE HAD TO DEVELOP TIMOTHY GOES TO SCHOOL AND
GET TIMOTHY AND FRIENDS MOVING OFF THE PAGES OF THE BOOKS, I ABSORBED MORE THAN
I EVER THOUGHT I COULD ABOUT A WHOLLY NEW ART FORM. THE INTRICATE WORKINGS,
INNUMERABLE DEPARTMENTS, AND HUGE PRODUCTION MACHINE THAT NELVANA IS JUST
AMAZED ME AND CONTINUES TO AMAZE ME AS WE TACKLE A WHOLE NEW SERIES. WHAT FUN!

ROSEMARY WELLS, AUTHOR

WHAT WAS IT LIKE WORKING WITH NELVANA? IT WAS ROCKIN'. THEY MADE THE WORLD THAT
I CREATED COME TO LIFE. IT WAS COMPLETELY TRUE TO WHAT I WANTED IT TO BE.

WILLIAM JOYCE, CREATOR OF ROLIE POLIE OLIE

THE THREE PRINCIPALS HAVE WORKED LONG AND HARD TO DEVELOP THE COMPANY TO WHERE
IT STANDS TODAY. IT'S A GREAT ACHIEVEMENT. FROM OUR POINT OF VIEW, NELVANA IS A
FABULOUS FIT WITH OUR KIDS' NETWORK AND OUR KIDS' FOCUS. THEY'VE GOT WORLD-CLASS
CHARACTERS AND THEY HAVE A GREAT REPUTATION AROUND THE WORLD. WE'VE TALKED TO
SOME U.S. PLAYERS AND THEY THINK CORUS'S RELATIONSHIP WITH NELVANA IS FABULOUS.

HARRIET SHAW, EXECUTIVE CHAIRMAN, CORUS ENTERTAINMENT

CHAPTER 3 THE 1990s

William Joyce is a popular children's author. Millions of kids delight in his stories about such characters as Dinosaur Bob. Like many writers, Joyce is loyal to print. He saw no need for his characters to migrate from the page to the television screen. Then, in 1997, a man named Toper Taylor changed his mind.

Taylor is president of Nelvana Communications Inc., of Los Angeles, Nelvana's U.S. subsidiary. When he spots a literary property that would translate well to the screen, he is reluctant to take no for an answer. Taylor called Joyce and said he wanted to fly to Shreveport, Louisiana, where Joyce lives, to explain to him why some of his characters should become TV stars. Joyce said he was not interested. Taylor said he would come anyway.

Joyce said, "I can't lock the Shreveport airport."

When Taylor arrived, he had a stroke of luck. The hotel he was booked into turned out to be a dump and, as a result, Joyce felt sorry for him.

Over the phone, Joyce said, "I'm still not interested but I feel bad about where you're staying. I'll take you for a drink."

Joyce came to get Taylor. They walked through the hotel's parking lot, carefully avoiding used hypoder-mic needles and other litter, went to a bar, and had a drink. Joyce still wasn't interested but he invited Taylor home to dinner anyway.

At Joyce's house, Taylor browsed through a stack of drawings, ideas that had yet to be turned into books.

Taylor said, "What's this robot thing?"

Joyce said, "That's Rolie Polie Olie."

Taylor said, "What is it?"

Joyce read him a poem about Rolie Polie Olie, a happy robot who lives on a planet of happy robots.

Taylor listened. Then he said, "Let me take a shot at showing you what we could do on television with this character."

A few weeks later, Taylor showed Joyce a sample of computer-generated 3-D animation portraying Rolie Polie Olie and his world. Joyce loved it. Within two years, *Rolie Polie Olie*, co-produced by Nelvana and a French company and animated in France and Vietnam, was on TV in 100 countries. *Entertainment Weekly* called it "the best new children's show" on TV and the *Hollywood Reporter* claimed, "Little else on television can match the sheer enchantment of *Rolie Polie Olie*." In the U.S., where the series appears on the Disney Channel, it won an Emmy Award.

GEORGE SHRINKS, A COLLABORATION WITH AUTHOR WILLIAM JOYCE, FOLLOWS THE ADVENTURES OF A MINIATURE BOY WHO LIVES WITH HIS NORMAL-SIZE FAMILY.

Nelvana began as a partnership of three creative people. Before long, other creative people—animators, painters, writers—joined the team, but the three founders continued to run things. But by the 1990s, the company had long since passed the stage at which three people could manage it. As it grew and matured into its third decade of existence, other talented executives—people like Toper Taylor and Emmanuèle Petry, producers Patricia Burns and Stephen Hodgins, computer animation specialist Scott Dyer, chief financial officer Sally Moyer Kent, and lawyer Harriet Reisman—were called on to play important roles.

Each of these people possesses special skills. One of Taylor's is finding promising literary properties and gaining the trust of their creators. During that first visit to Shreveport, he had to overcome Joyce's belief that TV could not faithfully render the world he creates in books. While adamant in this belief, Joyce did concede that, while he didn't like conventional cel animation, he was intrigued by computer animation. That gave Taylor the opening he needed.

Computer animation is not suitable for all subjects but it was a natural for a little robot from outer space. Joyce was also dubious about working with a large studio, fearing that the uniqueness of his work would not be respected. Taylor persuaded him that Nelvana doesn't operate that way, that a *Rolie Polie Olie* TV series would be a collaboration in which he would be fully involved.

Taylor was as good as his word: Joyce liked Nelvana well enough that he has since put another of his characters into the studio's hands. The new show, *George Shrinks*, is about a 10-year-old boy who is three inches tall. Despite his earlier misgivings, Joyce accepted that *George Shrinks* was better suited to cel animation than computer animation. "He trusts the production department now," explains Taylor. "And we've become very good friends."

During the 1980s, Nelvana engaged the big U.S. talent agency William Morris to help it drum up business. Taylor was the agent assigned to its account. He represented other animation companies as well, including such major ones as Hanna Barbera, whose 2,000 cartoon characters include the Flintstones and the Jetsons.

"I was a TV packaging agent," he explains. "That meant I would use the resources of the agency from the talent, literary, and publishing departments. I would combine those elements with Nelvana to create a package that we would bring to a U.S. network and sell. For example, I was Denise DiNovi's and Tim Burton's television agent. We put them together with Nelvana and sold *Beetlejuice* to ABC. I was one of Roseanne Barr's TV agents, and we put the two companies together and sold *Little Rosey* [a Nelvana-owned show]."

In 1989, Taylor decided he would rather be part of Nelvana than just its agent. "I left William Morris because I felt the TV business was becoming more international in scope," he says. "I felt comfortable that Nelvana could produce the series that I was involved in developing and selling. I wouldn't

have to worry about their execution of concepts developed by my office. I also felt that Michael Hirsh and Patrick Loubert were outstanding executives with a world of experience that I could learn from, and that there was an opportunity to take this small private company and turn it into a mini-major publicly traded studio."

His strategy to make Nelvana bigger was two-pronged—continue seeking out literary properties that would make good television, and get further access to U.S. networks for more Nelvana shows. Both goals coincided in Taylor's project to get a show based on Maurice Sendak's Little Bear character onto the Nickelodeon cable network. There were only two problems with this project—the key executive at Nickelodeon wasn't sure she wanted a Nelvana show, and Sendak, the renowned creator of *Where the Wild Things Are*, had been turning down proposals to put his work on TV for decades.

Nelvana had to be on Nickelodeon because specialty channels were driving the growth in demand for children's programming; whereas an on-air network might have four hours a week of children's shows, a specialty service filled all 168 hours in the week with them. The executive Taylor had to win over was Brown Johnson,

(LEFT) FROM ROLIE POLIE OLIE, CREATED BY WILLIAM JOYCE. DIRECTOR: MIKE FALLOWS. (BELOW) FROM GEORGE AND MARTHA.

During a lunch meeting, Brown mentioned to Taylor that the first book she had ever read was *Little Bear*. "I knew that if I delivered *Little Bear*, we would get the opportunity to work with her," Taylor says. He began to work his persuasive powers on Sendak. His timing was good. Sendak had been having a frustrating experience trying to develop movie projects. And he was a fan of Nelvana's work on *Babar*. Eventually, Taylor persuaded Sendak to change his mind about television and to approve a series based on Little Bear. The show debuted in 1995, has been running ever since on Nick Jr., and is seen in 130 other countries as well. A Little Bear feature film was completed in 2001.

Bringing Joyce and Sendak into the Nelvana fold were major steps. Even more important, from the point of view of expanding the company, was Taylor's success in securing exclusive access for Nelvana to important blocks of time on the CBS and PBS networks. Prime time for young children is Saturday morning and, in 1990, CBS had been the top-rated Saturday morning network, thanks largely to a show called *Teenage Mutant Ninja Turtles*. By 1997, however, CBS's Saturday morning schedule had fallen to the bottom of the ratings heap, mainly because the Federal

head of Nick Jr., Nickelodeon's programming for two- to five-year-olds. Johnson couldn't quite figure Nelvana out. On the one hand, it produced mass-market Saturday morning shows on the major networks, such shows as *Jim Lee's WildC.A.T. Covert Action Team*s and *Cadillacs and Dinosaurs*. Those weren't Nick Jr.'s style. On the other hand, it did *Babar*, a beautiful series but one with a European feel. That wasn't Nick Jr.'s style either.

Communications Commission (FCC) had ruled that every TV station had to air three hours of children's educational programming. Since Saturday morning was the only period during the week when CBS had children's programming, the network had to dedicate its entire schedule to educational programs, which drew smaller audiences than entertainment shows.

CBS had switched from cartoons to live action series to try to find educational programs kids would watch. But the ratings kept falling; as a result, the licence fee CBS could pay to a third party also kept falling. When it dropped below $100,000 an episode, a lot of potential producers lost interest.

This situation created an opening for Nelvana as a cost-efficient producer with a proven track record in creating entertaining kids' TV that qualifies as educational under FCC guidelines. What makes Franklin the turtle educational when Ninja turtles are not? The stories in *Franklin*, as in the other Nelvana pre-school shows, contain information that relates to the daily lives of small children; they try to teach kids important life lessons. Franklin, for example, faces problems familiar to the three- to seven-year-olds who watch the show—problems such as fear of the dark, going to

(LEFT) RILEY, STAR OF NELVANA'S PRIME-TIME SERIES "JOHN CALLAHAN'S QUADS." (BELOW) A DRAWING BY JOHN CALLAHAN.

Sorry, Lefty, you can't hold your liquor!

school, and making new friends—and solves them himself. Nelvana is able to submit to the FCC names and résumés of educational consultants who work on the shows as well as a report of the educational premises underlying each episode.

Taylor went to CBS and said that Nelvana could come to the network's rescue—but only if it was made the exclusive provider for a three-hour block of Saturday morning shows. Other companies also wanted this business, including DiC, the Jim Henson Company, and Universal.

Nelvana's advantage was that it already had programs that fit CBS's needs. Taylor met with the top executives of CBS and came out of the meeting with the deal, the first ever in which a network had turned an entire section of its schedule over to a third party.

Six Nelvana shows aired on CBS in September 1998: *Franklin, Anatole, Dumb Bunnies, Flying Rhino Junior High, Mythic Warriors,* and *Tales from the Cryptkeeper.* The result was that CBS's ratings doubled over the previous year. However, the shows aimed at older children, *Flying Rhino Junior High* and *Mythic Warriors,* did better than the pre-school programs.

In 2000, Nelvana launched a similar arrangement with PBS, the U.S. public network. PBS had never been a competitor in the Saturday morning children's TV sweepstakes. The three-year deal with Nelvana was for six half-hour shows of 13 episodes each for a total of 78 episodes, more programs than PBS had ever ordered from an individual company. The PBS deal required Nelvana to take on a new role as a television syndicator because PBS operates as a coalition of individual stations rather than as a conventional network. Two executives in Nelvana's Los Angeles office, Irene Weibel and Jill Newhouse-Calcaterra, had to make sure that every PBS station in the country was airing the programs in a time period that would result in the strongest possible ratings, Taylor explained. "We successfully launched in about 85 per cent of the country, which is terrific," he said. "And the ratings have been sterling."

Nelvana's deals with CBS and PBS received little attention in Canada, but because of their scope and novelty, they made the U.S. entertainment industry sit up and take notice. The deals, says Michael Hirsh, "really defined the company as a significant player that wasn't going to sell just a show at a time. Our competition sells a show at a time. Very few companies

TALES FROM THE CRYPTKEEPER

He thrilled you with his comic book. He chilled you with his live-action series. THE CRYPTKEEPER™ is back with a brand new animated series and a worldwide licensing program!

NELVANA

sell blocks of shows. Toper's initiative to secure that shelf space made people look at us differently—as a mini-network. If you're a rights owner and you've got a great character and you want to get into one of those time periods, we are a good player to talk to. It gave us a lot of leverage in the marketplace."

The deals were an example of the ability the company has shown throughout its history to overcome setbacks. In 1994, three years before the CBS deal, Nelvana had been the largest supplier of animation to the U.S. networks. Then Disney bought ABC and became the network's exclusive supplier of animated shows. And Saban Entertainment, a major competitor and the creator of *Mighty Morphin Power Rangers*, merged with the Fox network. To top it all off, NBC proceeded to get out of children's programs. This string of developments shut independent animation companies out of three of the four over-the-air networks in the U.S. Some independent animation companies went out of business as a result, but Nelvana survived by selling to cable companies and overseas broadcasters. Then, thanks to Taylor's two big deals, it was back on U.S. network television.

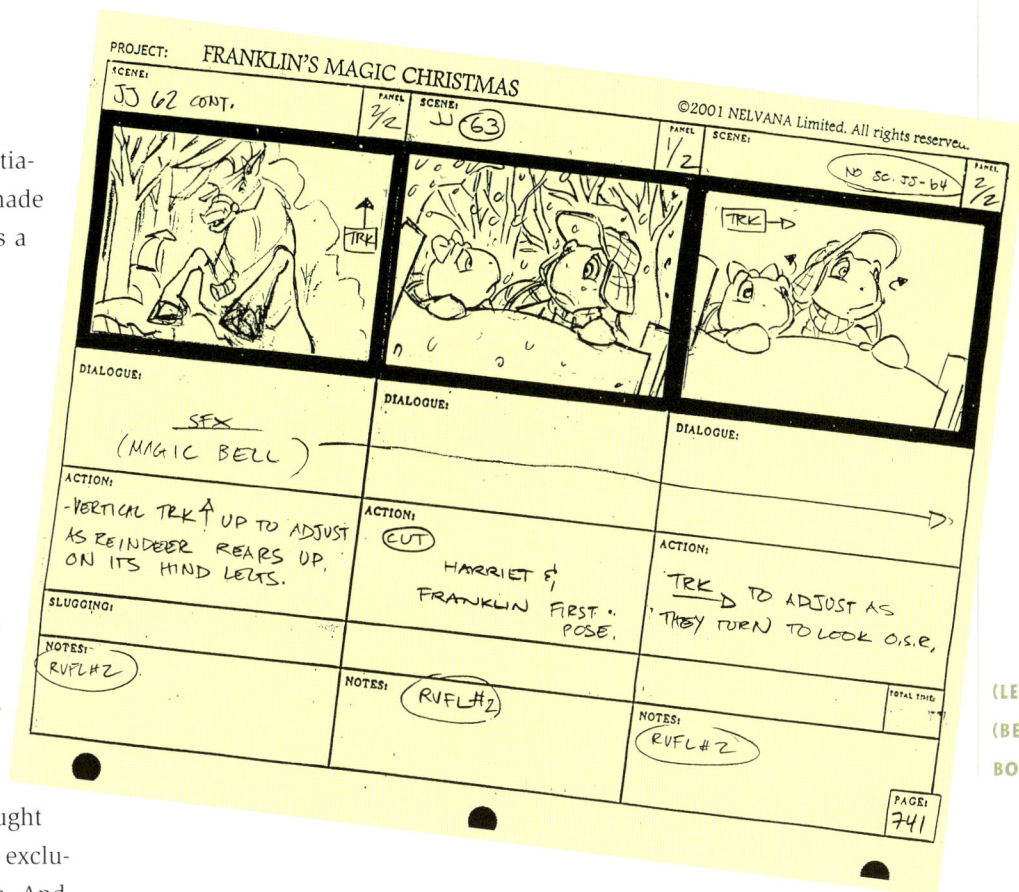

(LEFT) FRANKLIN STORY BOARD.
(BELOW) DUMB BUNNIES, BASED ON THE BOOKS BY DAV PILKEY, AIRED ON CBS.

There's more to success than just selling TV shows—you have to make sure you have the right show on the right station, as the case of *Franklin* demonstrates. *Franklin* is based on the phenomenally popular series of books written by Canadian author Paulette Bourgeois and illustrated by Brenda Clark. In 1995, Nelvana acquired the TV and merchandising rights. The TV series, launched in 1997, is broadcast in 147 countries. The problem was in the biggest of those countries, the U.S., where *Franklin* was the lowest-rated program on CBS.

"This is a very important property to Nelvana," explains Taylor. "It's a Canadian book that had sold 14 million copies worldwide. So it was unacceptable to have this kind of benchmark show performing so poorly. Nickelodeon called and said it was looking for a new preschool show immediately. We were able to navigate some very complicated waters and take *Franklin* off CBS and put it on Nickelodeon, replacing it on CBS with *Rupert*, which was just coming off Nickelodeon."

The result? Nickelodeon put *Franklin* on twice each morning, and within three weeks, it was the most watched pre-school show on its schedule and one of the three most watched cartoons on its entire schedule. *Franklin* holds the record for the highest-ever rating for a show on Nick Jr.

Why would a show that flopped on CBS be a hit on Nickelodeon? "Commercial broadcasters don't like pre-school programs," Taylor explains, "because the amount of money a pre-schooler has to spend as a consumer is significantly less than a nine-year- old has. CBS had been showing it at 7 or 8 a.m. At that hour, the HUT [house-holds using television] is very low."

Not only did Nickelodeon give *Franklin* a better time slot, it had more pre-school viewers than CBS to start with. "We put *Franklin* on a network that has the most kids watching it and it exploded out of the gate. That is why it is so important for independent programmers and producers to understand that the broad-caster does matter. Being in bed with the most important broadcasters is extremely valuable. Without that switch from CBS to Nickelodeon, *Franklin* as a merchandising property would be dead."

The travels of *Franklin* were not over. A year later, Viacom, owner of Nickelodeon, bought CBS and turned the CBS Saturday morning schedule over to Nickelodeon's control. As a result, CBS did not renew its deal with Nelvana. However, Nickelodeon kept *Franklin* on its own schedule and put it back on CBS as well. There, with the help of a better time slot and promotion on Nick Jr., it got twice the rating it had achieved before.

The 1990s were Nelvana's era of expansion. In 1989, the company moved to new quarters on Atlantic Avenue, in a dilapidated industrial area at the western edge of downtown Toronto. The new studio complex had 75,000 square feet, compared with only 40,000 in the previous studio. An annex, opened in 2001, provided an additional 32,000 square feet.

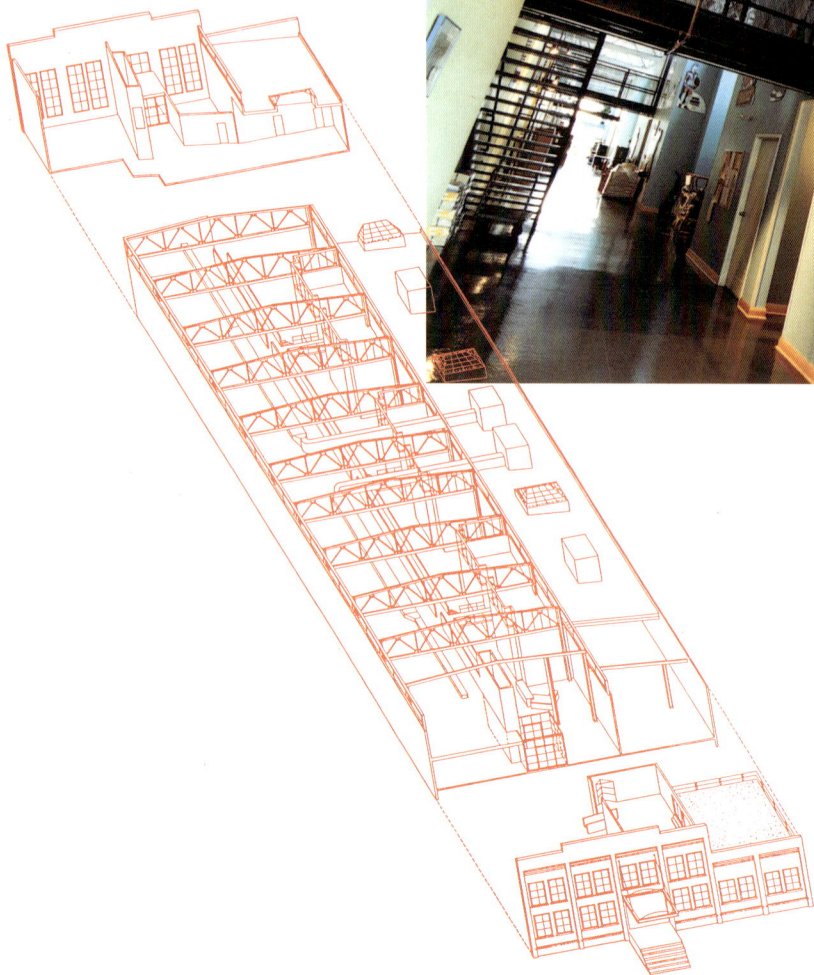

Patrick Loubert understands real estate and has a knack for spotting neighbourhoods on the way up. The Queens Quay building, with its rats, dark corridors, and overpowering food smells, was transformed, after Nelvana's departure, into the Terminal Warehouse, comprising expensive condos, offices, and shops. A similar transformation is happening in Nelvana's new neighbourhood.

"When we bought this building, it was a shell," Loubert recalls. "It was the cheapest building in the city, and the neighbourhood was awful. One morning, there was a dead body just up the street. Somebody had shot someone in a fight, and the body was still there when people came to work. After that, women were afraid to walk the two blocks to the streetcar."

But the building was a good deal, and Loubert could see that the area, with its convenient location and sturdy old industrial buildings, was ripe for redevelopment. Under the supervision of architect Bruce Kuwabara, Nelvana's building became a bright and airy workplace, featuring sandblasted brick walls and skylights. Colourful posters of Babar, Franklin, and the rest of the Nelvana crew add to the cheery atmosphere. Other creative enterprises, including YTV, the children's network, followed in Nelvana's pioneering footsteps, renovating other nearby buildings. Now a condo building boom is bringing thousands of new residents into the surrounding area.

The Toronto headquarters and nearby annex house 500 storyboard artists, layout artists, character designers, location and prop designers, background artists, in-betweeners, writers, story editors, computer animators, other animators, and various administrative workers.

Although much of the animation is co-produced with Asian companies, all the pre-production and post-production is done in Toronto, which makes the Nelvana headquarters there one of the world's biggest cartoon factories. During the 1990s, Nelvana turned out a constant stream of new titles. Not even veteran staffers can name them all. There was Scholastic's *The Magic School Bus* and *Stickin' Around* and *Blazing Dragons. Tales from the Cryptkeeper* and *Donkey Kong Country* and *Cadillacs and Dinosaurs. Ned's Newt* and *Redwall* and *Cardcaptors.* Some shows last for a year while more popular ones run for several years. The most successful of all last until 65 episodes have been made; that's the number needed for a program to go into syndication.

Nelvana continues to specialize in entertainment for pre-schoolers, but it has also made programs for other segments of the population. *Sam & Max,* based on a comic book of the same name about a dog and a rabbit who use their special powers to solve crimes, is aimed at older kids and adults. *Bob and Margaret* has a sophisticated brand of humour aimed mainly at adults. The show chronicles the adventures of a childless British married couple—he's a dentist, she's a chiropodist—as they go about their daily lives.

Screenwriter William Goldman once wrote that in the movie business,

"nobody knows anything," meaning that nobody knows before a movie opens whether it will be a hit or a flop. The same principle applies to television. *Bob and Margaret* is a good example. It's clever and funny and it had good reviews; moreover, in light of the success of *The Simpsons*, it's clear that an audience exists for adult-oriented animation. *Bob and Margaret* is a success—but only in Canada,

(ABOVE LEFT) THE OFFICES AND SPACES REFLECT THE NATURE OF THE COMPANY AND ARE FILLED WITH IMAGES AND ARTIFACTS FROM THE SHOWS. (LEFT) FROM REDWALL.

(RIGHT) BOB AND MARGARET, NELVANA'S FIRST PRIME-TIME COMEDY, WAS BASED ON THE SHORT FILM BOB'S BIRTHDAY, MADE AT THE NATIONAL FILM BOARD OF CANADA BY DAVID FINE AND ALISON SNOWDEN. SNOWDEN PROVIDED THE VOICE OF MARGARET. (BELOW) 13 EPISODES OF SAM & MAX WERE PRODUCED, BASED ON A CONCEPT BY STEVE PURCELL. DIRECTOR: STEVE WHITEHOUSE.

where it is the top-rated Canadian show on the Global network. It was dumped by Comedy Central in the U.S. and it flopped in Britain, even though the characters are British.

Nevertheless, for continuing success and growth, a film studio has to try new things; if it doesn't, an ever-changing marketplace will leave it behind. Moreover, to use a baseball analogy, the more times you step up to the plate, the more chances you have to hit a home run. "Because nobody knows what will be a hit, it makes sense to maximize your chances," says Nelvana treasurer John Vandervelde. So you produce as many shows as you can in the hopes that one of them will turn out to be that

elusive megahit. *Bob and Margaret* might have been but it wasn't. Maybe another one will be.

As part of its strategy of staying on top of new developments, Nelvana developed a 3-D animation division. The animation sample that induced William Joyce to entrust Rolie Polie Olie to Nelvana was produced by Windlight Studios, a Minneapolis 3-D animation company headed by Scott Dyer. Subsequently, Nelvana bought Windlight, and Dyer moved to Toronto to become Nelvana's vice-president of production and information technologies. By 2000, three shows, *Donkey Kong Country*, *Rolie Polie Olie*, and *Pecola,* had been created in 3-D.

A common misconception is that computer animation is cheaper than manual animation and, therefore, is bound eventually to replace it. This notion, says Dyer, is wrong. The computer can do certain things better than people can, but not everything, and the appearance of a computer-generated program is quite different from that of one made by traditional methods. In short, computer animation is a complement of, not a replacement for, traditional animation.

One of the most tedious and labour-intensive jobs in animation used to be painting the drawings. "The first thing Nelvana did was bring in digital ink and paint to paint the drawings," Dyer says. "We did that because it was much more efficient and resulted in a better product."

But when it comes to the animation itself, the decision whether to use computers (3-D) or manual (2-D) methods depends on the nature of the story and characters. *Rolie Polie Olie*, which is about robots in outer space, is perfectly suited to the futuristic look of 3-D. On the other hand, Dyer says, "*Little Bear* needs to be 2-D. *Babar* straddles the fence. I could easily imagine a 3-D version of *Babar*. It would have worked. It would have been different. Would it have been better? Probably not.

"It has to do with the complexity of the artwork, the shapes, the amount of detail, what the camera needs to do. Some shows are very static and the camera just shoots people talking; other shows, you want a swooping 3-D camera. You have to make your choice based on all that stuff."

While computers are a cost-efficient way to paint animated drawings, they are more expensive than traditional animation for creating the backgrounds to animated action. Here the difference between manual and computer animation is comparable to that, on a live action set, of building a re-creation of the Taj Mahal or just using

(LEFT) DONKEY KONG COUNTRY, NELVANA'S FIRST FORAY INTO COMPUTER ANIMATION, WAS BASED ON THE COMPUTER GAME OF THE SAME NAME. DIRECTOR: MIKE FALLOWS. (BELOW LEFT) NELVANA'S PRODUCTION IS RELIANT ON THE INTERNET. THE GLOBAL NATURE OF PRODUCTION REQUIRES THE COMPANY TO STAY CONNECTED TO ALL OF ITS SATELLITE OPERATIONS. PRODUCERS, ARTISTS, AND WRITERS POST PROGRESSIVE STAGES OF PRODUCTION ON THE NELVANA WEB SITE FOR OTHER TEAM MEMBERS.

a painting of it in the background. The animator using a computer has to construct everything in three dimensions—a laborious process. Once again, the nature of the show determines which technology is used. If the same sets are going to be used repeatedly, 3-D is a good option. Not so if there is a different background for each episode. "We tend not to pick shows that have a different setting each week because it's too expensive," Dyer says.

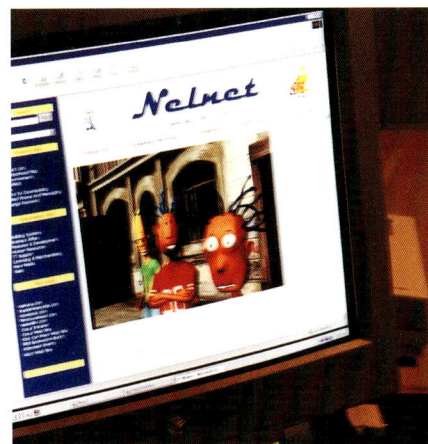

Dyer has always been fascinated by the arts but he became a computer programmer "because my parents thought you could only make money if you were in computers. I have always pursued the artistic side of computing. The best way to do that has always been through computer animation."

The continual advance of the technology makes it a fascinating field to work in. "It continues to march toward the ability to create things that can seamlessly integrate with live action. And the ability to create things that are real," says Dyer. But computerized characters aren't going to replace live ones any more than they are going to replace hand-drawn ones. Computer animation is "sort of in between animation and live action," Dyer says. "I don't think it's ever going to replace anything."

Acquiring good properties is a bit like big game fishing—success requires ingenuity, persistence, and luck. *Rolie Polie Olie, Babar,* and *Rupert* are examples of valuable properties that Nelvana reeled in. Curious George was one that got away. Yet Curious George and Nelvana were a perfect fit. Like Babar, Curious George is a children's classic with enduring appeal to each new generation. Created in the 1940s by Hans and Margaret Rey, the Curious George character is a monkey that lives with a "Man in a Yellow Hat." Curious George gets into endless scrapes, but the Man in the Yellow Hat always comes to the rescue. The artwork is delightful. Curious George seemed like a natural for adaptation to the screen.

Nelvana approached Margaret Rey in 1991. She was unreceptive. Curious George's only previous encounter with another medium had been as a character in "animatics," little drawings that are photographed. Margaret Rey had not been happy with the result. But, after much persuasion, Nelvana got her to sign a contract conditional upon Nelvana presenting her with satisfactory story proposals and drawings. "She thought we'd never get past the hurdles," says Hirsh. "But, to her surprise, we got past the literary hurdles."

The stumbling block was the artwork. The widow, then in her 80s, kept telling Hirsh, "George is real."

Hirsh replied, "What do you mean by that?"

She said, "George is a real monkey."

Hirsh said, "We've given you very realistic drawings of a monkey. We're going to treat him like a real monkey."

She sighed "You don't understand. George is real."

Margaret Rey finally admitted that the drawings were good but she was just not ready to let go. "She lived alone in Boston," Hirsh recalls. "Most of her friends had died. People constantly pursued her for the rights. It was a way of keeping busy. If she signed, she said, 'I'll never hear from you again.' Which was not true."

CADILLACS AND DINOSAURS WAS A SERIES BASED ON 1980S COMIC BOOKS BY MARK SCHULTZ.

So Nelvana had to drop Curious George. Then, a couple of years later, a young film-school graduate with no track record in the film business acquired the rights. As Hirsh heard the story, when Margaret Rey asked the film graduate what his idea for Curious George was, he said, "George is real."

Hirsh continues: "We interviewed him later to find out what he had done that we hadn't. He said he told her he wanted to do a live action film in which George was real and John Cleese was the Man in the Yellow Hat. For that idea, she gave him the rights without any approvals. Nobody enters into a contract like this. Our contract was worth more to her and her future estate. She gave it away for nothing. The young man realized he couldn't get it done, so he flipped it to Hanna Barbera, who flipped it to Ron Howard's company Imagine. The licensing rights ended up at Universal, where a movie has been in development for seven years, which may or may not get made. John Cleese may or may not be the Man in the Yellow Hat."

If Nelvana had obtained the rights, the curious monkey and his friend would long since have been on TV and might have starred in a movie as well. But you don't land every big fish you go after.

The credits at the end of a Nelvana program roll past too fast for most people to read them. That doesn't matter much since the audience for many of the shows hasn't yet learned to read. But for anyone with an interest in the globalization of the economy, the credits make interesting reading.

Take John Callahan's *Pelswick*, a show that made its debut in 2000. It's another of Toper Taylor's finds, the first animated series featuring a kid in a wheel-chair. John Callahan's *Pelswick* is the creation of John Callahan, a quadraplegic, recovering alcoholic who lives in Oregon. The

credits declare that this show is a "Canada-China co-production." Meanwhile, *Franklin*, Nelvana's most important Canadian property, is a Canada-France co-production.

The Canadian TV industry depends on co-production, a business formula that Nelvana helped to pioneer. The Canadian government has signed treaties with several countries whereby programs jointly produced by companies from the two countries qualify as domestic productions, thereby getting the preferential tax treatment afforded domestic producers. Of 19 productions Nelvana was committed to for

JOHN CALLAHAN'S PELSWICK IS BASED ON CHARACTERS CREATED BY JOHN CALLAHAN, THE CELEBRATED HUMOURIST-CARTOONIST WHO IS A QUADRAPLEGIC. JOHN CALLAHAN'S PELSWICK IS THE COMPANION SHOW TO "JOHN CALLAHAN'S QUADS," A PRIME-TIME SERIES. THE CARTOONIST SENT IN PAGES SUCH AS THIS DURING THE DEVELOPMENT PHASE.

2000–2001, all but two of them had foreign partners.

These partners include companies in France, Japan, China, Germany, the Philippines, and Australia. The predominance of Asian co-producers reflects the maturing of the Asian animation industry. Some of the same companies that started as subcontractors providing low-cost animation labour have developed since into producers. "The co-production treaty was one of the financing methodologies that Canada put into place that is very important to the industry's growth because it was a way of sharing the risk," explains Hirsh. "Since you always end up [doing animation] in Asia, why not co-produce with Asia? It's more logical than having a European co-producer. But we also want to keep doing European-content shows, so we try to balance European and Asian co-productions."

The person most closely involved in this balancing act is Patricia Burns, vice-president of production, a Nelvana veteran who first worked for the company in the days of *Rock & Rule*. Burns was making so many flights between Toronto and Europe that she decided she'd be better off working out of the Paris office. She moved to the French capital in 1998. The European location is also advantageous for keeping in contact with Asia by phone, since the time difference is only six hours, less than half that from Eastern Canada.

"Our ability to work sometimes in four countries on one production and pull it off is one of our greatest strengths," she says.

In addition to co-productions, another financing method has been important in spurring the growth of the Canadian film industry—the

able tax regime, it is doubtful that Canada would have grown, in the years since Nelvana was founded, into the second biggest exporter of TV shows in the world, after the U.S.

Because of the global nature of its business—both producing and selling shows all over the world—Nelvana has had to continue to hone its skills at navigating cultural differences. The Turkish objection that *Babar* was excessively non-violent was just one of many examples. The objection to Scholastic's *The Magic School Bus* was another. In this educational show, kids go on adventures aboard a big yellow school bus. The program was a hit in both Canada and the U.S., but at first, no other country would touch it, even though it was an excellent show that seemed to have universal appeal. "Turns out," says Taylor, "that there are no big yellow school buses in other countries."

Happily, this problem was not insoluble. To gain acceptance in France, explains Emmanuèle Petry, "I just took out the word 'school.' So in France, the show is called *Le Bus Magique*. It's not a school bus, it's just a magic yellow bus."

Another barrier to acceptance of the show, says Taylor, was that Europeans did not want to be educated by North Americans. They felt their

system whereby producers can earn tax credits by putting money into Canadian productions. In 1999, Nelvana collected $6.4 million worth of tax credits from the two levels of government. The rationale of this policy is that everyone benefits—film companies grow, new jobs are created, and because of income and other taxes generated by film productions, the public treasury collects more money than it forgoes. Without the favour-

education systems were far superior, so they were insulted by an educational program. After two years of huge success on PBS, however, other countries were lining up to get Scholastic's *The Magic School Bus*, and it wound up being seen in 143 countries.

Translating programs from English into dozens of other languages creates other kinds of problems. Some shows lose more in translation than others. A case in point is *Dumb Bunnies*, which contains a lot of humour dependent on word play. For example:

Mama: Let's make cookies.
Baby: Fantastic.
Mama: We need flour. Would you get some flour?
Baby: Sure.
[She goes out and brings in some roses.]
Or:
Papa [driving down street]: Let's go to Disneyland.
[We see a sign that says Disneyland—Left.]
Papa: Disneyland left. I don't know where it went.

How do you translate scenes like those into French or German? You don't, because the word games work only in English. So, whereas some shows survive translation intact, *Dumb Bunnies* has to be substantially rewritten.

In the case of *Rupert the Bear*, the language problems revolved around accent. Rupert is English, so obviously he has an English accent. But, given that the show is aimed at other anglophone countries in addition to Britain, how English should the accent be? Rupert is played by a Canadian actress, Julie Lemieux, who voices the part with a mid-Atlantic accent. Both Scottish television and the *Daily Express* were involved in choosing the voice, recalls Patricia Burns. "They understood that Rupert had to have global appeal. Canadians can understand a British accent, but when we were selling *Rupert*, one of the comments in the U.S. was 'Oh, it's very British,' as if that were a bad thing."

Such cultural problems are amplified by the fact that most Nelvana shows are co-productions. Petry, who sells programs throughout Europe, deals with cultural issues on a regular basis. "Because the cultures are different, the needs are not always the same," she explains. "Sometimes the age target is different. We had that problem on *Anatole*, where M6 [the French broadcaster] wanted it to be for six- to 10-year-olds and we wanted it to be pre-school. We were pulling our hair out trying to make the stories work for both. Eventually M6 pulled out."

Nelvana is a North American company, its biggest market is the U.S., and the Los Angeles office, headed by an American, plays a major role in determining the company's roster of programs. "For Nelvana, style is associated with the creator, and most of the creators happen to live in the U.S.," says Toper Taylor. "It has been our objective to create programs which work around the world, but which culturally speak to the child in North America. The U.S. is an elusive marketplace for international companies. We've succeeded beyond our expectations. We have more television shows on the air than Disney and Warner combined."

That's great for Nelvana's U.S. operation but it complicates life for the group operating out of Paris. "A lot of Europeans say our shows look too American," says Petry. "That's extremely difficult to address because it's everything and nothing at the same time. What does it mean? If it's too violent or the colours are too bright, that's easy to fix. But not if it's overall. *Rescue Heroes* looked too American. 'The jaws are too large. The feet are too large. They have too many muscles.' Then the Americans say, 'No, they're fine, they're heroes—they have to have muscles.' You go around in circles trying to find a solution when it's a cultural thing."

Petry's most difficult challenge was with *Mythic Warriors*, a program based on the Greek myths. "In North America," she recalls, "they wanted the actual myths but at the same time they wanted it for children. So we had to take out a lot of the myths that were too violent. And they wanted to change some of the meanings. There is the one in which Oedipus sleeps with his mother and kills his father. In France, they wanted to be absolutely loyal to the original myths, but then it couldn't be on TV in North America because it wasn't politically correct. Then at some point, one of the partners wanted to have a host introduce the shows and the other one didn't. Then they switched positions—one wanted the host but the other one didn't anymore. It was a nightmare."

The show did make it to air, however, in 95 countries. And Nelvana even managed to solve the Oedipus problem. How? "We left it out," says Petry.

In that case, no compromise was possible but, usually, co-producers manage to find a way to resolve their differences. Compromise, however, can create problems of a different kind. "When there are too many partners in Europe between France and Germany and the U.K., we call it Europudding," says Petry. "It has no flavour, taste, vision. Designers are frustrated because their original design has been tortured. That's the toughest part."

Something like that happened with *Pippi Longstocking*, based on a series of books by Swedish author Astrid Lindgren about a spunky young girl. Nelvana co-produced a feature about Pippi in 1997, followed by 26 episodes of a TV series. The feature starred, among others, the voices of Catherine O'Hara and Dave Thomas. Clive Smith directed the movie, which Nelvana co-produced with Svensk Filmindustri, of Sweden, and Trickompany, of Germany. "In a true

co-production," Smith says, "each country has both financial and creative involvement. So it becomes very much a diplomatic process."

In the case of *Pippi*, the negotiations revolved around the Swedes' desire to retain the character of the original book and Nelvana's attempt to broaden its appeal to non-Swedes who had never heard of Pippi. There was a fundamental problem in the plot of the original story: the villain, Miss Priscillious, the town busybody, wasn't bad enough. "For there to be a story," Smith says, "there has to be a challenge, there has to be vulnerability and a threat. Life-threatening? Why not? Well, not according to the Swedes. 'We've got to realize that Miss Priscillious is not a bad woman,' they said. Well, if she's not a bad woman, we don't have a story. Look at any fairy tale. If you don't put your hero or heroine right in the fire and have that person come out triumphantly, the audience isn't going to feel satisfied.

"I made Miss Priscillious as bad as I could. I would have made her 'badder'. But I got her at least to a point where, even inadvertently, she put Pippi in danger. That was the compromise. It wasn't her will, but because of her actions, we managed to get Pippi in a life-threatening situation.

(LEFT) NELVANA'S THEATRICAL FEATURE PIPPI LONGSTOCKING, DIRECTED BY CLIVE SMITH, WAS A THREE-WAY CO-PRODUCTION WITH SVENSK FILMINDUSTRI AND TRICKOMPANY. THE SUBSEQUENT TELEVISION SERIES WAS DIRECTED BY PAUL RILEY. ART: FRANK NISSEN. (BELOW) PIPPI'S NEMESIS, MISS PRISCILLIOUS.

"The other thing was Pippi herself. The lead character needs to be multidimensional, needs to be sad, happy, worried, for us to relate to her. That is what storytelling is all about. Well, according to my friends in Sweden, Pippi was always happy, she didn't get sad or worried, she just skated over the surface of life and it barely touched her. This is our main character; you can't do that. But Pippi is a property that was so well known in Sweden. You can't change it completely, because then why do Pippi?"

In the original story, Pippi's father, a sea captain, falls overboard and floats away. To Smith's dismay, Pippi isn't concerned about it. I didn't want to make it the thread of the story, but can't we have a moment where she remembers her father? I did get that in. I also wanted a song about it. But they said, 'Oh no, that would be too sad.'"

Then there are the stories that just don't travel at all, despite their popularity in their native countries. *Marsupilami* is a French comic book about a half-cat, half-tiger with a long tail. Disney created a TV show based on it and it failed. *Bécassine* is a French comic strip from the 1930s about a nursemaid in Brittany who wears a white apron and clogs. She has been a favourite of generations of French children. "Everybody loves her," says Petry, noting that *Bécassine* merchandise sells well in France. "Michael wanted to do something with her, but she doesn't travel. Even in the company, nobody could understand it."

Jim Weatherford, the son of an American father and Japanese mother, grew up in the U.S. but has spent all his working life in Japan. Operating out of Nelvana's Tokyo office, he sells programs across the Asia Pacific region and, like Petry, has to grapple with the fact that animation from North America sometimes seems alien to his customers. For example, a character that is supposed to be about eight years old in a North American program seems closer to 15 to a Japanese audience. "He's bigger, and the face is much more defined. Kids mature faster in the West."

Shows such as *Little Bear* and *Franklin* are a harder sell in Asia. "What's considered cute in North America is not necessarily considered cute in Japan," Weatherford says. However, both shows are running in Japan, and the kids like the stories despite the lesser appeal of the characters. However, Nelvana's adult show, *Bob and Margaret*, is unsaleable in Asia because it is too "socially specific." And *Maggie and the Ferocious Beast* is a non-starter in the Islamic countries in Weatherford's territory because one of the characters, Hamilton, is a pig, which is considered unclean.

Burns agrees that Asian broadcasters are "very picky about the pro-

gramming that they will buy. The Asian co-producers have to be careful about what agreements they enter into because they may find they don't have a market for the show, particularly an adult-audience show. For example, most of the Chinese companies buy their programming from Japan. What sells is action stuff based on comic books. The softer North American pre-school programs sell in some markets but not in others. It's a tough territory to predict."

A safe prediction is that Asia, with its vast population, will be an increasingly important market for Nelvana in the future. But, as other companies in other industries have discovered, success there doesn't happen overnight. As of 2001, Nelvana's

revenues for any one of its programs in all of Asia were less than the same program could earn in a single major European country such as Italy or Germany.

Some successful entrepreneurs can't wait to take their companies public. Selling shares has two big advantages for the owners of a private company: it gives them a chance to get rich and it gives them a chance to expand their business. At Nelvana, the idea was first discussed in 1993, but the three founding partners weren't enthusiastic about it. When they started Nelvana in 1971, they had been, in Hirsh's words, "three hippies who knew next to nothing about business." Now they were experienced in business but knew little about the complexities of running a public company. Moreover, they were used to thinking of Nelvana as theirs; if they took it public, it would no longer be all theirs.

On the other hand, the company hadn't been entirely theirs for a long time. In 1983, they had given up 25 per cent of their shares to the investors who loaned them the money to finish *Rock & Rule*. Although they had repurchased most of those shares, the Nelvana board had ever since included directors from outside the company. Still, having Nelvana shares listed on the Toronto Stock Exchange would be a major step. "Your life changes when you become a public company," says Loubert. "You have to be careful what you say, how you con-

duct yourself. Your legal department has to tell you yes, no, maybe, and you have to listen to them. You can't play as fast and loose as when you were a private company."

When Nelvana finally took the plunge in 1994 and made an initial public offering (IPO) of $30 million in shares, it was done reluctantly, and more as a defensive move than out of a desire to make the company much bigger. Three other major Canadian film companies, Alliance, Cinar, and Atlantis, had already issued shares. "With our peers going public," explains Hirsh, "our concern was that without the same available capital, we would find new players entering the animation field and we would suffer. We were doing well as a private company but we were concerned about how we would continue to perform in

a competitive environment. We had to be well capitalized and we had to be able to offer our employees and key staff share options."

The company had probably gone as far as it could go as a partnership; going public was necessary to take it to the next level. But it was a step that Nelvana was not well prepared to make. Because of its lack of preparedness, the company was launched into a period of turmoil that would last for almost three years. The problem was

twofold. First, Nelvana lacked a well-thought-out business strategy to take advantage of the new capital it would raise by selling shares. Second, its internal organization and management practices were inadequate.

The business strategy that should have been adopted immediately upon raising money from the public was to get out of service work entirely and return to the more profitable propri-etary production that would allow the company to build its most valuable asset—its program library. During its first decade, Nelvana did mostly pro-prietary production, but after it went into debt in 1983, it had been forced to switch to service work. At the time of the 1994 share offering, there was a 50-50 split between the two. It wasn't until 1996 that service work was drop-ped altogether, a step that, in retro-spect, should have been taken in 1994.

In addition, Hirsh believes it was an error not to expand more rapidly after the initial share offering. "If we had gone all proprietary and put the money to work in the first year, we could have been back in the market the first year raising more money," he says. "You want to go through the money you raise and do your next deal pretty quickly. We didn't know that. We were under the impression that it was better if we didn't have to dilute investors right away and we could make this money last as long as possible. Some of our peers went out there and did offering after offering. We didn't."

However, such a strategy might have been difficult to implement given the internal disarray that afflicted the company subsequent to the IPO. Before going public, Hirsh and Loubert had shared overall management as co-CEOs. A clear division of labour existed between them, with Loubert responsible for overseeing production as well as generally making the place run, and Hirsh concentrating on sales, marketing, and Nelvana's outside relationships. Clive Smith had been vice-president in charge of program development. Smith also ran Bear Spots, Nelvana's television commercial division, until the company closed it down in 1995.

When the company went public, management decided to drop the co-CEO system in favour of a more conventional structure, with Hirsh as chairman, Loubert president, and Smith executive vice-president. This system didn't work because the other executives didn't know who they were supposed to report to. And while Hirsh and Loubert had collaborated

(LEFT) BETTY AND MICKEY PARASKEVIS CREATED MAGGIE AND THE FEROCIOUS BEAST. (BELOW) TRADITIONAL BACKGROUND ARTIST'S PALETTE.

well under the old system, they often disagreed under the new one. Exacerbating the situation was their failure to recruit executives with the knowledge and skills required to run a public company.

"The problem was that we didn't have a senior financial person in the company," Loubert says. "Michael was handling distribution and marketing, and I was handling production. Eleanor Olmsted [the chief operating officer and general counsel] was not a finance person but a lawyer, and a very good one. The problems that cropped up continually in the public

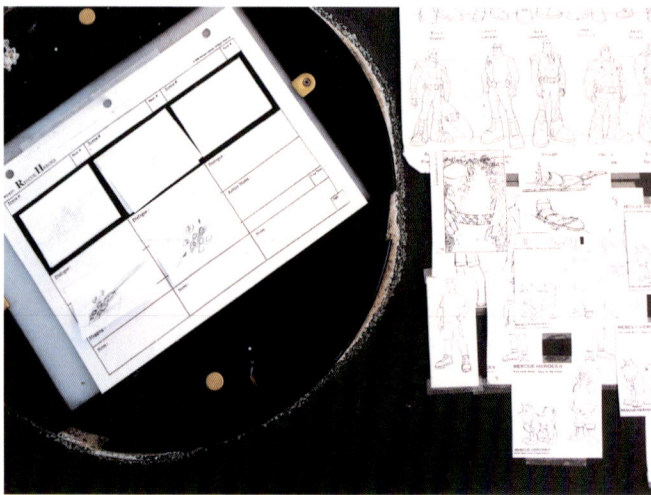

finance and chief financial officer, thinks the deal was probably a non-starter from the beginning because Nelvana was too disorganized at the time. "They didn't have the information the acquirer wanted organized in a fashion that anyone could make sense of," she says.

Hirsh changed his mind about the deal and considered making a bid for the company on his own, but Loubert and Smith continued discussions with Golden Books. "It was a real mess," Loubert recalls. The stock market helped to resolve the situation by pushing the price of Nelvana's stock higher than Golden Books wanted to pay. A contributing factor was that, because of the favourable tax treatment accorded Canadian investors in film production, Nelvana was worth less to foreign owners than to Canadian ones.

When Hirsh looks back on the Golden Books affair, he sees it as one more example of how the three partners have been able to overcome adversity each time they were confronted with it. Looking at the company's history as if it were a screenplay, he says, "Nelvana is the story of three partners sticking together through thick and thin. It's more interesting that we had this big test. Every story has to have its dark cloud, and this was the dark cloud."

company structure none of us had the answers for, and when that happens, there's a lot of fighting over answers."

The low point was an abortive attempt to sell the company to a U.S. publisher, Golden Books. Hirsh had initiated the deal, and Loubert recalls that, at the time, "it seemed to make a lot of sense. We were having a lot of arguments over who had responsibility for what and how much work had to be done. Selling the company looked like it was the only solution."

Sally Moyer Kent, who arrived in 1997 as senior vice-president of

Placing two fingers a fraction apart, he adds: "We were this far from self-destructing."

As in the movies, just when things look their darkest, someone comes to the rescue. In this case, it was a man named Stuart Sucherman, who runs a small U.S.-based management consulting firm specializing in the entertainment industry. Sucherman, who was recommended to Nelvana by Gerry Leybourne, then CEO of Nickelodeon, is what Hirsh calls a "corporate therapist."

"The only way to understand organizations is to understand chaos theory," Sucherman says. "Every organization has its problems and its difficulties and its personality disputes and its dysfunctionality. That's why I have a business."

Chaos theory is especially appropriate to organizations in the entertainment business, he adds, because they are more difficult to manage than companies in other industries. "Normal people don't get attracted to the entertainment industry," he explains. "In show business, the stranger you are, the more successful you are."

It didn't take Sucherman long to discover what was wrong at Nelvana. "There was divisiveness. There was a confusion in roles. There was a tremendous amount of distrust. It had

reached a point where it was destroying the company. It was unravelling and there was a real issue about whether Nelvana was going to survive.

"The three of them were not businessmen. Michael was as close as any but he really wasn't. Patrick saw himself as a creative guy, and Clive wanted to direct movies. Another problem was a disconnect between the creative people in Toronto and the L.A. office that was generating a lot of the deals. There was almost disdain for the stuff that Toper was trying to do and a lack of understanding about how hard it was."

(LEFT) FROM "MARVIN." (BELOW) BACKGROUNDS ARE CREATED USING A VARIETY OF METHODS. HERE MELISSA GRAHAM PAINTS A TRADITIONAL MINIATURE COLOUR SKETCH TO BE USED AS A REFERENCE FOR THE FINAL, FULL-SIZE BACKGROUND.

which we knew about," he says. "We desperately needed a true chief financial officer."

What happened to Nelvana is typical of the growing pains that often afflict successful companies. Because they are successful, these companies get bigger and more complex, thereby rendering the skills of the people who started them inadequate to the task of managing them. "You see it a lot in the dot-com area and in creative businesses," says Sucherman. For him, what was unusual about Nelvana was that its problems were on the organizational side rather than the creative; it's usually the other way around.

"The hard part in this business is creating something. The easy part is running something. To create something that makes money and is good— I'm in awe of that. We are usually trying to fix that piece of it. And that wasn't a problem at Nelvana. It wasn't that they were turning out crap and not making any money."

Like Hirsh and others in the business, Sucherman sometimes compares real life to the movies. "They are all interesting characters," he says. "You couldn't write characters like this. Patrick: the brooding artist. Michael: very entrepreneurial, a little wild-eyed. Clive: the artist who just wants to paint his pictures.

Sucherman interviewed the partners and other executives and also met with the board. Then he recommended that Hirsh and Loubert go back to the old co-CEO structure that had worked in the past and recruit new executives to run the company's financial and legal affairs.

Michael Harrison, who was a member of the board at the time, says Sucherman didn't tell the board anything it didn't already know. "He didn't do very much except focus the board on the management problem,

"The fact the three are still together says a lot about who they are and the deep-seated nature of their relationships. They are all good guys. There are no villains here. When you say 'Nelvana' to people in this business, it means something. It has a great image of being very creative and successful. They are an institution, not just a company."

The problems had been big but the solution was simple. As Sucherman had recommended, Hirsh and Loubert went back to being co-CEOs, with their responsibilities clearly demarcated. Smith remained senior executive vice-president and Harrison became chairman of the board. Sally Moyer Kent was recruited to be chief financial officer, beginning in 1997, and Harriet Reisman arrived in 2000 as general counsel.

These changes unleashed the potential of Nelvana, triggering a growth spurt that continues to the present. In the four years since the executive deck was shuffled, the re-energized company's revenues and operating profit have quadrupled. While Loubert oversees production, Hirsh concentrates on sales, and Smith spearheads various creative projects, Sally Moyer Kent fine-tunes the business operations.

The advantage of bringing in someone from the outside is that she is not wedded to doing things the way they have always been done at the company. As Nelvana had grown up over the years, new legal entities had been created as new initiatives were launched. By the time Moyer Kent arrived, there were 20 of these entities. But she looked at the company from a fresh perspective and saw that Nelvana was not in 20 businesses but in only two. One was production and distribution, the other was branded consumer products. So she reorganized the accounts to reflect that reality.

The simplified structure enhances the company's ability to operate effectively and to plan for the future. "Before you couldn't say, 'How is mechandising doing?' Instead, you'd get this sliver and that sliver, with different people doing the accounting for these different entities. Everybody worked hard. There was a lot of attention to detail. But the big picture was missing."

Business planning, budgeting, cash management forecasting, and monthly reporting systems were all upgraded to public company standards. Moyer Kent's goal was to get rid of all remnants of the old financial planning system, which dated back

(LEFT) THE LARGE, OPEN ENVIRONMENT OF THE PRODUCTION FACILITY ENCOURAGES TRADITIONAL ART TECHNIQUES TO LIVE ALONGSIDE COMPUTER TECHNOLOGY. (BELOW) FROM ROLIE POLIE OLIE.

to the days of *Mr. Pencil* and *Zounds of Music*, a system based on the question, "Oh my God, where are we going to get the money we need tomorrow?"

Receivables come in slowly in the entertainment business, but that is no excuse for living on the financial edge, Moyer Kent says. "You have to have a forecast. If your business is selling shows, you've got to have a system that tracks when your receivables are coming in and when you are going to spend the money. You run the company in the aggregate as a business, figuring how much you are going to need and how to raise the money. Every year we got better. 2001 is the first year we have a mechanism in place to forecast the cash on a monthly and quarterly basis."

To make this happen, and to finance the move to all-proprietary production, the company needed better access to credit. Previously, it had loans attached to each individual production. Moyer Kent told the Royal Bank she wanted an overall line of credit based on a business plan encompassing all the company's production activities. "We ended up expanding our credit substantially, which gave us more capital to grow and more confidence that we could continue to push the business without going bankrupt," she says.

As of 2001, Nelvana had a credit line of $200 million, compared with about $10 million five years before. More credit plus the influx of equity from the share offering finally made the shift to 100 per cent proprietary production a reality. "If you are doing 100 per cent proprietary, you require more capital," says Moyer Kent. "We spend $120 million to deliver our production slate. That's a lot of money when only 50 per cent of the cash comes in during Year 1. You have to find a way to finance it as an overall pool."

In addition to finance, Moyer Kent's major interest is acquisitions. Since arriving at Nelvana, she has helped finalize the deal to acquire Windlight, the Minneapolis 3-D company, and has worked on the purchases of two publishing companies, Kids Can Press, of Toronto, and Klutz, of Palo Alto, California. These purchases made Nelvana the leading children's book publisher in Canada and one of the top 10 in the U.S. Since so many

(OPPOSITE PAGE) FROM FRANKLIN. (ABOVE) STORYBOARDS ARE CONSTANTLY REVISED BEFORE FINAL APPROVAL. (LEFT) CHRIS KATOPODIS, STORYBOARD REVISION ARTIST, 2001.

of Nelvana's characters originate in books, publishing was a natural extension of its business. In the case of Kids Can, acquired in 1998, both companies were already in the *Franklin* business. Kids Can had sold 25 million copies of Franklin books worldwide by 1998, and the turtle was starring in one of Nelvana's most popular shows.

PUBLISHING

With the success of Babar, it was probably inevitable that Nelvana would wind up in the publishing business. The international appeal of the movies and TV shows about the famous elephant demonstrated that bringing great books to life is what the company does best. Many other Nelvana shows since then have been adapted from European and North American literary properties, both classic and modern. "Since so many of our projects begin as books, it makes sense for us to own book companies," explains Michael Hirsh. That's why Nelvana purchased Kids Can, Canada's largest children's publisher, in 1998. Two years later, it bought Klutz, a publisher based in Palo Alto, California, that specializes in how-to books for kids. With these two acquisitions, Nelvana became one of the 10 largest children's publishers in North America. Kids Can's biggest asset is Franklin the turtle, a creation of writer Paulette Bourgeois and artist Brenda Clark. Since 1986, the Franklin books have sold over 30 million copies, in more than a dozen languages. Kids Can also publishes dozens of other titles, fiction and nonfiction, for every age group, from preschool to teens.

Kids Can licensed TV rights to Franklin to Nelvana in 1995. That was when Hirsh first raised the subject of a buyout with Kids Can's partners, Valerie Hussey and Ricky Englander. "We said, 'Yes, we're open to selling, but let's work together for a little while and see how we get along,'" Hussey recalls. By the time a deal was finalized two years later, "we had worked with them long enough and felt quite comfortable," she says. Englander left Kids Can after the sale, while Hussey stayed on as president and CEO. She takes part in Nelvana's development meetings, which give her useful insights into what sorts of stories the world is looking for. "I have been in the publishing business almost 30 years, so for me this is an opportunity to learn all sorts of new things," she says.

When Kids Can is considering a new submission from an author, is it now more conscious of the story's adaptability to the screen? "Absolutely," says Hussey. "We look at everything with a broader eye and ask, 'What is the potential, and if there is potential, what do we have to do to maximize it?' But that doesn't prevent us from publishing books that won't translate [to the screen]. Our publishing philosophy, strategy, and mix have not changed. We've always done some risky high-end publishing, but it is paid for by broad commercial publishing in the best sense."

Another change is that Kids Can, if it is interested in a property, is now more likely to offer a three-book contract, rather than one, just in case Nelvana is interested. In addition to Franklin, Andrea Beck's Elliot Moose has also become a Nelvana character. There will be more to come, and there's always the possibility that something that starts out as a Nelvana show will be adapted into a Kids Can book.

Klutz is a different kind of company because none of its books have characters. Three Stanford University students, John Cassidy, Darrell Lorentzen, and B.C. Rimbeaux, started it in 1977. They began by selling sidewalk juggling lessons along with three no-bounce beanbags. After a week's efforts, they had earned $35. This impressed them so much that they decided to turn their juggling lessons into a book. Cassidy, the English major, wrote the book. Lorentzen, the business major, wrote the business plan, and Rimbeaux, who was studying psychology, applied for the bank loan.

That first book, *Juggling for the Complete Klutz*, is still in print and has sold two million copies. It comes with three beanbags. Dozens of other how-to books followed, packaged with such tools of their trades as face paints and yo-yos. Explains Cassidy: "We think people learn best through their hands, nose, feet, mouth, and ears. Then their eyes. So we design multisensory books." Like those of Kids Can, Klutz's products have enjoyed international success. They are available in 19 countries.

Why would Nelvana, which is known for its famous characters, want to own a publisher that does not create characters? "Nelvana is about being an aggregator of children's brands," explains Hirsh. "We wanted to have a brand that is not a character brand and we are starting to look at licensing and merchandising it. I think Klutz is a big enough brand to eventually be a TV network. The shows on it could be anything from quiz shows to how-to shows to cartoon shows." It seems that big things lie ahead for Kids Can and Klutz as Nelvana works toward its goal of becoming the leading independent children's entertainment company in the world.

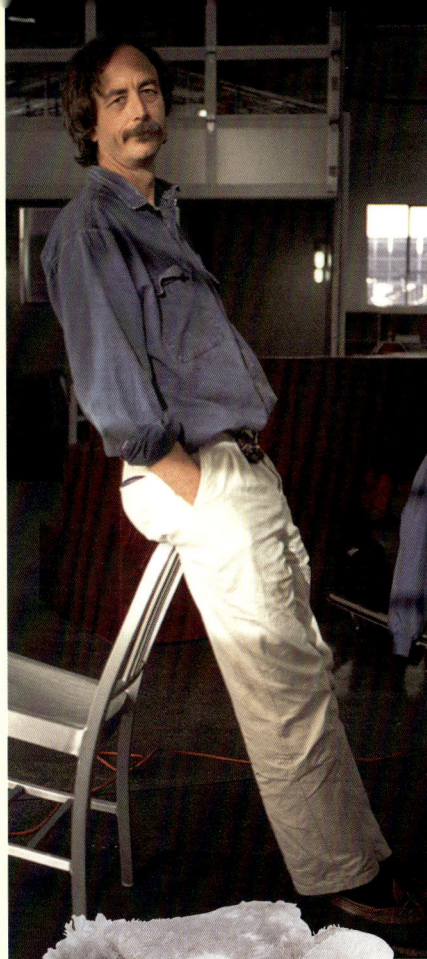

(LEFT) JOHN CASSIDY, KLUTZ PRESS. (BELOW) THE INNOVATIVE SLAPPIES, FROM KLUTZ PRESS.

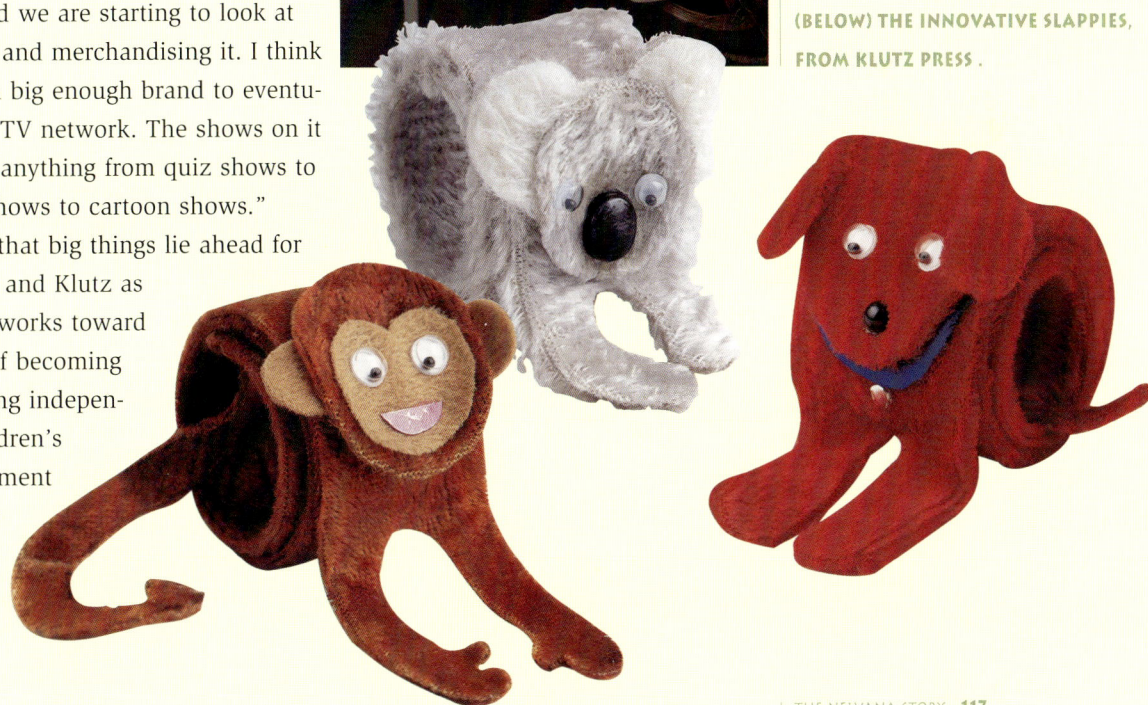

Moyer Kent reports to both Loubert and Hirsh. It's an unusual management structure but it works. "You have to get a consensus," she says. "They are very different and they balance each other out."

Nelvana would have been better armed financially to seek acquisitions had not the stock market consistently undervalued its shares. Fortunately for its shareholders, however, the stock did perform better than those of the other Canadian entertainment companies. And in September 2000, investors in Nelvana's first share offering, who had paid $14 per share, were well rewarded for their patience. Corus Entertainment Inc. of Toronto announced it was buying Nelvana to create a global children's broadcasting and production powerhouse. Nelvana would continue to operate as Nelvana, with its management intact, but it would now be a unit of Corus rather than an independent company. The price was $48 per share, for a total of $600 million.

At the press conference announcing the takeover, John Cassaday, president of Corus, described Nelvana as a "Canadian jewel." Why did the majority shareholders who had created this jewel decide to sell it?

"It's about taking Nelvana to the next level," explains Michael Hirsh. "Being part of Corus gives us vertical integration, where we are both broadcaster and producer. Our relationships with worldwide players are going to be stronger because we are a stronger player.

"It was also a soft landing for the partnership. One of the things about partnerships is figuring out an exit strategy. Even though it was a public company, it was run as a partnership, and they are hard to maintain. I think we did exceptionally well maintaining it for 30 years. But the sale to Corus allows the partnership to de facto end. Now we're part of a larger group and the company can grow the way that it needs to rather than service the needs of the individual partners.

"There are horror stories of endings of partnerships. What happened to us four years ago could have been one of them. This is a nice ending to a great story, and now there's a new beginning because we are part of this bigger entity."

For Loubert, the deal with Corus is "a much better fit" than a takeover by Golden Books would have been. He too sees an exciting future because "I think that Corus wants to use us as an expansion vehicle." Meanwhile, it was business as usual. "We're planning productions, planning expansions, and looking at acquisitions the same as we were before. They were always subject to the board and now they'll be subject to another board [that of Corus]."

For Michael Harrison, the deal means he is relieved of his duties as Nelvana's chairman since Nelvana no longer needs its own board of directors. But he enthusiastically backed the deal. "You cannot compete on a world-scale basis in that industry unless you can demonstrate that you've got the financial wherewithal to complete a project. This allows them to breathe a little easier. They are not going to have access to unlimited amounts of money, but this allows them the comfort of knowing that they can now look at projects

without having the very confining guidelines that the board imposed on them. It gives them the opportunity to go for not necessarily more expensive projects, but better projects."

Sally Moyer Kent, who gained experience in mergers and acquisitions during a previous job with investment dealer Morgan Stanley in New York, believes it was the right time to sell for several reasons: the company was big enough and successful enough to be attractive to a buyer, there was a healthy market for acquisitions in the

investment in Teletoon [a Canadian cartoon channel]. Now we're not only integrated with a broadcaster, we have much deeper pockets for acquisitions."

The word most often used to describe Nelvana at the beginning of the first decade of the new century is "focussed." It is focussed because, after 30 years, it has finally figured out what it is—an international company that creates its own animated programs for young children based on the world's best collection of cartoon characters, both classic and modern. Nelvana is unique in the international animation business in the depth and quality of its collection of characters. Even the behemoth Disney can't compare. Disney owns Winnie the Pooh, but most of its other famous characters are in the public domain, meaning that the copyright on the original works has expired. Anybody could make a show about Snow White, but only Nelvana could make a show about Babar.

The gallery of characters will never be complete. Lots more are on their way to the world's TV screens. In 2001, shows were in various stages of development based on such classics as Dr. Dolittle (the one who can talk to animals), Puff the Magic Dragon, and Heidi, as well as modern favourites such as Max and Ruby,

industry, and the shareholders deserved to be rewarded. To understand why the deal is good for all concerned, she suggests comparing it with what might have happened had a foreign buyer—Disney, for example—bought Nelvana. Such a buyer, she suggests, would have closed down Nelvana's offices, dumped its employees, and kept only the program library.

Instead, she says, "The employees have a future in a company that has a real growth opportunity. You couldn't have picked a better owner for them

than Corus. It's Canadian, they don't have any of their own facilities, so they need ours, they will invest in the industry, they keep the tax credits." And whether it is under the current management or another, Nelvana is going to continue to grow. "Nelvana has money now. It's great for the long-term strategy of the company. It was clear that Nelvana had to be in broadcasting. Look at Warner Brothers, Disney, Viacom, Fox—they all own production and distribution. We had no broadcasting except a minority

by the popular writer and illustrator Rosemary Wells.

The other thing that sets Nelvana apart is the absence of a recognizable house style, which is related to its expertise in faithfully bringing great books to life. If Disney did a show based on Maurice Sendak's Little Bear character, it would look like a Disney show because all Disney shows look like Disney shows. When Nelvana does *Little Bear*, it looks like a work by Maurice Sendak.

"You can't point to the television and say, 'That's a Nelvana show,'" says Toper Taylor. "That's never been our goal. But hopefully you can point to the television and say, 'I know that book. I've read that book.'"

If Nelvana in 2001 was focussed on the creative side, it was also focussed on the business side. Patrick Loubert, who financed the launch of the company on the $5,000 limit of a credit card he didn't ask for and who still has nightmares about meeting the payroll, knows better than anyone how far Nelvana has come. "Everything is more focussed now," he says. "There is a debate about strategy all the time. But financial controls are in place now that weren't in place before. There is a financial model, there are planning models, models for green-lighting pictures

(LEFT) FROM "ELLIOT MOOSE," A SERIES BASED ON THE BOOKS BY ANDREA BECK, PUBLISHED BY KIDS CAN PRESS. (BELOW) NELVANA OFFICES, 2001.

when we have enough sales to make them. We have far more fiscal responsibility than we ever had before."

So where does this focussed company go from here? Everybody sees bigger and better things ahead. "Nelvana's got nowhere to go but up," says Patricia Burns, who, like other members of the senior management team, believes the link with Corus will propel the company's growth. "You are going to see the natural connection between the distribution arm and the content arm," says Scott Dyer. "That's going to allow both sides to expand and allow new opportunities that we would never have had."

For Patrick Loubert, the future means more features. Nelvana already has *Care Bears*, *Pippi Longstocking,* and other features in its library, but Loubert wants a much longer list. "This studio has always created properties from the bottom up, but most other studios have created properties from the top down. By that I mean that they create feature films first and from them come the television shows and the merchandising. I would like for us to be able to do it both ways. It's harder to hold on to your senior artists as they mature and get better if all you're offering them is television."

Something else Loubert wants more of is live action. "Right from the beginning the studio has always been in live action," he points out. "What we are going to do now is take it a little more seriously because we have an owner who needs live action for YTV [Corus's children's network]."

Whether in live action or animation, Nelvana's founders were determined to continue producing fresh and original work. "We are very proud of *Pelswick*, the first show with a kid in a wheelchair as the protagonist," says Hirsh. "We want to continue to break down barriers and be innovators in our field. That's of critical importance to us—to be pioneers and keep the medium exciting."

Clive Smith foresees a growing divide in the film industry between low-budget, "guerrilla-like" filmmaking, on the one hand, and big-budget theatrical films, on the other. Underlying this trend is the fragmentation of the entertainment market among hundreds of TV channels and millions of Internet sites. Fragmentation reduces the licence fees a company like Nelvana can demand from broadcasters. "Because there is less money to work with, people are becoming more and more innovative," Smith says. "It's opening up a new world of production for people who can sit down in front of a laptop and produce a half hour of animation. This technology is allowing a renegade industry to open up. So in the future, you will have a very diverse landscape, ranging from innovative, stylized, low-budget productions, which may be distributed over the Internet, to big features that will come out in theatres."

Where does Nelvana fit in this scenario? "I think we'll be doing both. I am anxious to launch some features with a large budget so that we can do some of the things that we've dreamt of doing. On the other hand, we have hundreds of very creative, skilled, and diverse talents roaming the halls of Nelvana, and we should support individual endeavours by them."

(OPPOSITE PAGE) FROM MAURICE SENDAK'S SEVEN LITTLE MONSTERS.
(LEFT) COLIN MCMAHON IN THE SOUND DEPARTMENT ANALYZES A DIALOGUE TRACK FOR THE ANIMATOR'S REFERENCE.
(BELOW) FROM "BIRDZ," CREATED BY LARRY JACOBS, A LONG-TIME NELVANA DIRECTOR AND ANIMATOR.

As this intriguing future unfolds, a key asset will be Nelvana's many veteran employees, the ones Patricia Burns calls "the anchor people. They know the history. They are the ones you can go to when you are bringing in new people, when you need answers to problems. We have them in all departments."

Nelvana has grown from a three-man show to a small firm with a familial atmosphere to a large international corporation. But, for veterans like Burns, in one important way it hasn't changed: "Before, it was such a small company, with Michael, Patrick, and Clive being the guys. We all just hung on their every word and learned everything we could from them. Still to this day, although the company is huge and there are vice-presidents everywhere, you find that the older people will still go back to those guys. They were the inspiration and they had the knowledge, and they still do."

Michael Harrison, who was with Nelvana as an investor, adviser, director, and elder statesman from the days of *Rock & Rule* until the Corus takeover, considers the relationship a high point in his career. "I guess the association for me was so wonderful because it was so completely different from anything you run across in your day-to-day stockbrokerage life," he says. "Here were these goofy guys just spitting ideas, constantly having another brainwave."

And yet the Nelvana partners proved to be creative businessmen as well as creative artists. "They tried many ideas that didn't work, so they had to write off the development costs," recalls Harrison. "*Rock & Rule* was for teenagers. Now they are making shows for the two- to five-year-olds. They have come down to the audience that they found they could do best with. They are not stubborn. They flow with the times."

They are mellower perhaps but still ambitious, older but still enthusiastic. All three of them share their offices with posters and toys of their beloved characters. An oversized Babar doll peers down at Hirsh as he works the phones, overseeing a company that has offices in six countries and that sells programs in an incredible total of 180 countries, which is more than anyone can name. "One of my mottos," says Hirsh, only partly in jest, "is world domination through animation."

A childlike statement? Perhaps, but when you are running an anima-tion company and your customers are three-year-olds, the ability to make childlike statements is not necessarily a bad thing.

"What is just extraordinary to watch is that they still understand that market," says Harrison. "It's fascinating to watch three people go from their 20s to their 50s and still be able to think like kids."

One of the best things about youth is that the future seems full of promise. And it still seems that way for the seasoned kids at the helm of Nelvana. The company greeted the new millennium as the largest inde-pendent children's animation company in the world. (In the movie business, "independent" means not part of a major U.S. entertainment conglomer-ate.) As Nelvana celebrated its 30th anniversary, it was full of plans to add more live action to its production mix, to make more feature films, and to expand its publishing and merchandis-ing businesses.

Nelvana, in short, wasn't satisfied being merely the largest independent animation company in the world. "We will try to become," vows Hirsh, "the leading independent children's enter-tainment company in the world."